# Discourse on Policy-Making

# Discourse on Policy-Making

# American Foreign Policy

## Volume 10
Exxon Education Foundation Series
on Rhetoric and Political Discourse

### Edited by
# Kenneth W. Thompson

The White Burkett Miller Center of Public Affairs
University of Virginia

University Press of America

Lanham • New York • London

The Miller Center

University of Virginia

Copyright © 1987 by
University Press of America,® Inc.

4720 Boston Way
Lanham, MD 20706

3 Henrietta Street
London WC2E 8LU England

British Cataloging in Publication Information Available

**Library of Congress Cataloging-in-Publication Data**

Discourse on policy-making.

(Exxon Education Foundation series on rhetoric
and political discourse ; v. 10)
1. United States—Foreign relations administration.
2. Separation of powers—United States  I. Thompson,
Kenneth W., 1921-      II. White Burkett Miller
Center.  III. Series.
JX1706.A4  1987      353.0089      87-10446
ISBN 0-8191-6338-4 (alk. paper)
ISBN 0-8191-6339-2 (pbk. : alk. paper)

The views expressed by the author(s) of this publication do not necessarily
represent the opinions of the Miller Center. We hold to Jefferson's dictum that:
"Truth is the proper and sufficient antagonist to error, and has nothing
to fear from the conflict, unless by human interposition, disarmed
of her natural weapons, free argument and debate."

Co-published by arrangement with
The White Burkett Miller Center of Public Affairs,
University of Virginia

All University Press of America books are produced on acid-free
paper which exceeds the minimum standards set by the National
Historical Publications and Records Commission.

*Dedicated
to
Louis J. Halle
historian and philosopher
of policy-making*

*Dedicated*
*to*
*three generous donors*
*The Henry Thielbars*
*and*
*Mrs. C. H. Merriman, Jr.*

# Preface

The policy-making process in the United States is often seen in one-dimensional terms. We say the President is responsible for foreign policy. We view the secretary of the treasury or the Council of Economic Advisors as custodians of economic policy-making. The Congress holds "the power of the purse" through its influence over authorizations and appropriations. The Constitution determines policy-making.

Yet we recognize that this view of policy-making is too simplistic. It ignores relationships and interconnections. It overlooks the bargaining and negotiations that go on between the branches of government. It forgets that the founding fathers were ambivalent about the precise locus of responsibility for important aspects of policy-making such as foreign policy. It misconceives the view of human nature and man's "lesser motives" that inspired the founders to fashion a constitutional system of checks and balances.

Therefore, it is appropriate that such basic issues provide the framework for a volume on Discourse and Policy-making. Advocates of constitutional reform notwithstanding, a continuous dialogue and discourse go on at every level of policy-making. Indeed, the historical and philosophical questions discussed earlier in this series reach their most profound level of formulation and application in contemporary policy-making, for their resolution and accommodation in foreign policy has implications for the survival of mankind that extend far beyond the narrower lessons of any historical precedent.

Thus discourse on policy-making has consequences that weigh more heavily on the consciences of responsible men and women than have any of the difficult and baffling choices that have gone before. This fact makes discourse on policy-making a central issue of our time.

# Table of Contents

# Introduction

The debate over a government of separation of powers and one based on the so-called parliamentary model of the fusion of powers occupies some of America's best minds and most activist thinkers. In communities across the country books and study papers are being written, colloquia and regional meetings are being held. These inquiries can be fruitful in bringing greater understanding of the American political system and illuminating the possibilities of change and reform. They help the citizenry to focus on the structure of government as distinct from a continuing debate over policy.

A companion effort aimed at improving the understanding of the American system of governance throws the spotlight on a particular sector of policy-making. As an example of this approach, the present volume examines foreign policy. It seeks not so much to offer change as to preserve continuity. It rests on the proposition that governance and policy-making are more a result of shared responsibility and communication than of one all-determining locus of responsibility. Complexity of problems requires a measure at least of complexity in the fashioning of policy-making machinery.

The argument which can be made for including such an inquiry in a series of publications on political discourse is that the powers and duties of government in foreign policy-making are located in diverse centers of decision-making and the interrelation of such centers is properly a focus for studying foreign policy. The diffusion and decentralization of policy-making is a comparatively recent development. Louis J. Halle in discussing foreign policy and the dynamics of bureaucracy contrasts methods today with the mode of political discourse in Woodrow Wilson's era. We are reminded that Wilson retreated to the privacy of his family quarters in preparing his great documents of statecraft. Discourse past and present is the story of the growing bureaucratization of decision-making. Whereas Wilson called on a single respected newsman to assist him in writing the speech

which called on Congress in the spring of 1917 to declare war
against Germany, President Truman had the assistance of hundreds of aides in the preparation of the Truman Doctrine. With the
multiplication of the parties involved comes the need for more
effective communications and discourse. Halle strikes a balance
sheet of the advantages and disadvantages of the old and new
forms of discourse and suggests the growing need for understanding of those involved.

The next two chapters examine the relationship of the National Security Council and the historic longtime centers of
foreign policy responsibility such as the Department of State. I.
M. Destler analyzes some of the changes that have occurred over
time in staffing the government for foreign policy-making. He
describes the nature of personnel and the patterns of personnel in
the Truman and Eisenhower administrations and compares them
with more recent administrations. He shows how an early emphasis on discourse within administrations that maintained strong
centers of career service within a framework of centrist policy
orientation has shifted as foreign policy has been increasingly
politicized. Philip Odeen, who directed a major review of foreign
policy-making in the Carter administration, is concerned to demonstrate the increased complexity of the problems with which
administrations must cope and the apparent breakdown of coordination and followup in the last two administrations. He discusses
the dual role of the National Security Council which functions
both as personal staff to the president and in its institutional role.
The NSC staff is there to serve the president and its staff
functions are influenced by the requirements of individual presidents and NSC assistants. It also has four institutional roles:
developing security policy (including setting priorities), forcing
decisions on key issues, managing the decision process and
providing for followup, and providing the president with the
information he requires for decision-making. At each step along
the way the first need is for communication. For example, the
president must know what the constituent agencies in the process
consider to be essential. If the NSC assistant chooses not to
engage in the necessary discourse to gain the information from
the leading departments or if he fails to pass it on to the president,
the process envisaged by the National Security Act is aborted.
Throughout, policy-making assumes discourse and communica-

tions. In the 1980's, such discourse is more complex and complicated because the problems to be resolved are more complex. They are no longer, if they ever were, one-dimensional. They involve not diplomatic, military or economic issues but a merging of many combinations of all these issues.

Foreign policy-making also involves a determination of the major threat to the nation's security and preparing the necessary defense or deterrence against such a threat. This question is the theme of former Secretary of Defense James R. Schlesinger's "Discourse on the Threat." He examines the different conclusions we and the Europeans have reached on the threat to the West. He cautions against premature judgments as to the threat. It is his main conclusion that we must learn as a nation to live not with supremacy militarily and economically but with certain forms of parity. Presented earlier, his reflections are equally relevant for the rest of the twentieth century.

Former Secretary of State Dean Rusk concludes the discussion with a penetrating analysis of the constitutional and philosophical foundations of the idea of separation of powers as it affects foreign policy. If any attribute of American government highlights the essential role of discourse and communication it is the separation of powers. Secretary Rusk gives concrete examples of the many vital areas within which communication between the executive branch and Congress are necessary: meetings by the Secretary with leaders of Congress, breakfast sessions with State Department officials for from 60 to 300 concerned congressmen, congressional testimony and hearings and introducing the constituents of congressmen to the historic setting of the eighth floor of the State Department. Rusk makes plain that discourse, dialogue and communication are not only useful. They are utterly essential in a government that rests on the separation of powers.

PART ONE

# Discourse Past and Present

# Foreign Policy and the Dynamics of Bureaucracy*

LOUIS J. HALLE

*M*r. *Thompson:* Louis Halle was a research professor in the Woodrow Wilson Department of Government and Foreign Affairs in the 1950s, and he has continued to return to Virginia. He has many friends here. Others may not know him personally but know his writings. He was educated at Harvard in both undergraduate and graduate studies. At the height of the Depression he took a job with the Central American Railways in Guatemala and El Salvador; he returned to a position in the publishing business in New York City for Longmans, Green & Company. He then began a thirteen-year career in 1941 in the Department of State. His career was interrupted during that period but he worked mainly in inter-American affairs in the State Department. He was a member of the policy planning staff under George F. Kennan and Paul Nitze in a period that many considered the golden age of the policy planning staff.

He then took up residency in 1957 in Geneva and taught at the Graduate Institute of International Studies; ultimately, he became a Swiss citizen and participated prominently in such things as the founding of the International Institute of Strategic Studies. His writings include some twenty books. The Miller Center recently published his little classic, *The Elements of International Strategy.* Another book, *The Taking of the Philippines,* is in press, and a third book is in preparation. His *magnum opus* is *Out of Chaos,* an undertaking that shows that at least one social scientist dares to venture into the realm of natural science without too much fear of the consequences. It's a magnificent effort to try to weld together ideas in the natural sciences and concepts of philosophy to developments in the social sciences. He wrote *Civilization and Foreign Policy* when he had a rather passive

*Presented at the Miller Center on June 19, 1985.

assignment, as bureaucrats are wont to have from time to time, sitting at a desk in the State Department. He has written other books such as *Dream and Reality* that grapple with the problem of the relationship between ideals and reality. His *Men and Nations* is another widely heralded study.

Today we thought it would benefit all of us for him to look in a different way at the whole problem of the conduct of foreign policy under the title of "Foreign Policy and the Dynamics of Bureaucracy." Louis Halle, as he will tell us, means more by bureaucracy than usually intended in conventional writings.

*Mr. Halle:* I can't tell you how gratifying it is to come back here after thirty-one years of absence and see so many familiar faces and find that none of us have changed a bit. When Ken Thompson invited me to open this discussion for which we have assembled here this morning, I had vividly in mind, and I therefore proposed to Ken a thesis that I wanted to put before this group for its consideration and comment. It is a thesis about which I don't feel dogmatic at all, a thesis that I would like to see developed and thought out to a degree that I have not done.

The thesis has to do with the role that is played today in the shaping of foreign policy by what we may call "the dynamics of bureaucracy." Implicit in my concern with this question was the assumption that the foreign policy of a great bureaucratic government in the second half of the twentieth century is at least limited, if it is not entirely determined, by the bureaucracy rather than by individuals as such. Now this statement of mine is much too crude. It requires complication and refinement. And the complication and refinement that I will give it in the course of these introductory remarks will also be too crude and require complication and refinement.

I have for some time now found myself much concerned with the limitations that the dynamics of bureaucracy impose on the intellectual sophistication with which foreign policy is developed. So the problem that I want to set before you for discussion is that of the role played by bureaucracy and by bureaucratic procedures in the shaping of foreign policy.

In historical perspective this problem, which I shall be defining in due course, is of remarkably recent date, having arisen within the limits of my own lifetime. (I might say that I am old enough so that I saw Woodrow Wilson in the flesh. In fact, I am old enough so that I once listened to a speech by an earlier President, Theodore Roosevelt. I don't quite go back to George Washington, but a good deal of the distance.)

When I came to the State Department in 1941 it still had much of the character, a sort of remnant character at least, of an elite club in which everyone knew everyone else. In fact, I knew one foreign service officer who could put a face to every name in the foreign service and a name to every face. So personal relationships tended to prevail over such bureaucratic relationships as are represented by the flow-charts of the administrative experts, with their boxes and lines and so on. This didn't count; it was more a matter of personal relationships. Formal organization was at a minimum and was not always followed or taken seriously. Individuals tended to become associated with subjects or functions for which they showed a taste or an aptitude. (To take a personal example, I tended to become associated with speech writing. I wasn't a speech writer but I liked this kind of thing, so that I was always doing it.) Personal aptitude and tastes counted for a good deal. There was here, as well, something similar to the "old boy" network in former British governments, composed as those governments were, of men who had all gone to school together.

Moreover, before World War II the State Department had no arrangements for liaison at all with the War and Navy Departments, or perhaps with any other departments of the government. The State Department had a very good formal organization of liaison with the British, the French, the Siamese—you name them—but none at all with the War or Navy Departments. I'm tempted to tell very briefly how, during the middle of the war, this liaison was finally established by General Marshall in the Pentagon, who called in General Hull one day and said, "You know, on the other side of the river there is an organization called the State Department that is supposed to be responsible for the foreign relations of the United States. It is run by a man with your name, he is called Hull. We've never had any relations with him at all and I want you to cross the river, go over there, make an appointment with Mr. Hull, and see if you can't establish diplomatic relations between the War and Navy Departments and the State Department." So Hull went across the river and established diplomatic relations with us in the State Department.

The President of the United States before World War I, in his development and his conduct of foreign affairs, had always, I believe, depended on informal personal connections rather than on any bureaucratic apparatus. If he had to deliver a public address, he wrote it out himself, perhaps without consulting anyone at all. Professional speech writers had not yet been invented. And when President Wilson wanted to send an official message to Ambassador Walter Page in London, he wrote it out on his own little typewriter and then handed it to his wife for encoding. (He must have had a secretary—it's hard to believe that he didn't have a secretary—but he handed it to his wife.) And, as you know, when he became sick toward the end of his time as President, Mrs. Wilson ran the White House. Things were informal in those days, and personal. This had advantages but was not altogether advantageous; there were disadvantages, too. Wilson would send this message to Ambassador Page, with his wife encoding it, not paying any attention to the State Department at all, as if the State Department didn't exist. There was no need for bureaucrats, in other words, or for the apparatus of bureaucracy. All of this is very well described by Ray Stannard Baker in the several volumes of his biography of Woodrow Wilson.

Let me now cite one notable but not untypical example. It had been the personal policy of President Wilson to keep the United States out of World War I. This was the very center of his policy; it was almost a matter of religion for him to keep the United States out of World War I so that, at the end, it would be in a position to organize a new peace.

And this was his policy whatever the Secretary of State or anyone else might say. Indeed, Secretary of State Robert Lansing was not consulted, and was repulsed when he tried to get the President's ear. President Wilson was not the kind of man who was easy to tell anything to. You couldn't argue with him; he had his own views. And he didn't consult Lansing—and if Lansing had a different view about the war, and I believe he did, Wilson didn't listen to him; he paid no attention to him.

Finally, however, in the spring of 1917 the German government's policy of unrestricted submarine warfare defeated Wilson's determination to keep the United States above the battle, leaving him no choice but to lead the United States into the war on the side of the Allies.

How, then, did Wilson go about doing this? Did he call a meeting of the Cabinet? Or did he assemble all the concerned members of the Cabinet? Or did he set up ad hoc committees for the production of papers on this and that aspect of the situation? Did he order teams of speech writers into action? Nothing of the sort at all. The fact is that, for ten days before he asked the Congress to declare war, President Wilson remained alone in his bedroom almost all the time; he didn't even go to his office in the White House. He remained alone in his bedroom, I suppose pacing up and down. Day and night he saw virtually no one. Then, on the night before he went up the Hill to ask the Congress for a declaration of war, he sat down all by himself, before this little typewriter of his, and began to compose the address to the Congress.

At a certain point in this process of solitary composition—Ray Stannard Baker describes this very well—Wilson did feel the need to discuss the matter with some sympathetic soul. So what did he do? Did he send for the secretary of state? Did he send for the secretary of war? (Obviously the secretary of war ought to have had something to say about this.) Or did he send for any other member of the government at all? No, he sent for an old personal friend in New York, Frank Cobb, the editor of the *New York World,* and Frank Cobb rushed down to Washington, and when Cobb arrived at the White House at one o'clock in the morning of April 2, 1917, he found the President all alone, pecking out on his typewriter the address that he was to make before the Congress that very day. And this was the notable address (notable to my mind) in which he said, "We have no quarrel with the German people," insisting that the enemy was, rather, the imperial German regime that had no basis in their suffrage.

This, to my mind, was a very statesmanlike position. And that address of his is an address to put alongside Lincoln's Second Inaugural Address, which must have been composed in similar fashion, though without a typewriter—Lincoln writing it out on paper, crossing out this word, adding that. But perhaps, in the case of Lincoln's Second Inaugural, without even a Frank Cobb in his office.

So it was that the President of the United States, consulting no one in the executive branch at all or the legislative branch as far as I know, took the United States into the First World War. The absence of bureaucratic procedures was total.

Contrast this with President Truman's address of March 12, 1947, setting forth the "Truman Doctrine," finally reversing forever the American policy of isolationism and worldwide irresponsibility, if you will. Contrast this with Truman's address as reported by Joseph Jones in his book *The Fifteen Weeks*. (Joseph Jones had a hand in all this.)

Hundreds of bureaucrats, perhaps thousands—conceivably thousands, but hundreds at least—were involved for weeks through a great complex of State, War, and Navy committees and subcommittees. We called them "SWNC" committees. (I recall that I was on something like a subcommittee of a subcommittee of a supercommittee of the "SWNC" committee in this case, and I finally got so disgusted that I no longer attended its meetings.) All these bureaucrats were involved for weeks in this great complex of committees, plus a regiment of professional speech writers of whom Joseph Jones was one. What resulted, as we all know, was a speech that was to set, as I say, the whole foreign policy of the United States on a new course. (This speech, I may say, was not one to put beside Lincoln's Second Inaugural.)

I say again that the totally unbureaucratic world in which Woodrow Wilson operated does not belong to some distant past, on the scale of history—it belongs within my lifetime. I do not defend for a moment the kind of personal government represented by Wilson, and I believe by all presidents before him, nor do I think this kind of personal government, which had its element of irresponsibility, could have lasted. Beginning, however, in the 1930s, Washington has gone increasingly to the opposite extreme in faithful obedience to Parkinson's Law. (I hope you are all familiar with *Parkinson's Law* which is *the* greatest document in political science that has ever been. And I say that seriously. The first chapter of the book was originally an anonymous essay in *The Economist* on "Parkinson's Law." Every student of politics should know this first chapter and should know it by heart.)

Even before I left Washington in the middle 1950s, every move of the president in the foreign policy field tended to be the end product of whole complexes of committees and subcommittees and supercommittees locked in the daily struggle to make policy by the combinations and compromises of bureaucratic procedures. The president's statements became highly incoherent verbal messes—and I mean incoherent in the sense that one sentence didn't lead to the next or emerge from the previous one because everybody contributed a sentence, and then they juggled them. The president's statements became these incoherent verbal messes laced with public relations phrases composed on Madison Avenue, or composed in the spirit of Madison Avenue, that were intended to go down in history but did not do so.

Since we are fated, now, to be subject alike to the advantages and disadvantages of such bureaucratic government, we had better try to understand the dynamics of bureaucracy which now produces foreign policy in Washington—and no less so, I am sure, in Moscow. In fact, I have reason to know that the same kind of thing happens in Moscow, so everything that I say would apply no less to Moscow than it would to Washington.

Let me begin by presenting, as if it were a law of nature, what I conceive to be one of the principles that governs a great bureaucracy. Whenever a nation like the United States is at war, whether it's a cold war or a hot war, the competition for place and influence in the governing bureaucracy favors those who do not "underestimate the enemy." This is a fundamental point that I'm making now. The competition for place and influence favors those who do not "underestimate the enemy" in these situations of tense conflict of cold or hot wars. The competition for place and influence favors those who are not so "unrealistic," who are not so given to "wishful thinking" as to doubt that the threat posed by the enemy requires the most extreme measures if the nation, and if civilization itself, is to be saved from ultimate defeat. This, in the present limited context, is what I have essentially in mind when I talk of "the dynamics of bureaucracy." It's the dynamics of bureaucracy in situations of intense international conflict or war.

In the bureaucratic competition for place and influence, the hard-liners have the advantage over the soft-liners; the "hawks" have the advantage over the "doves." They have the advantage

when the nation is involved in such tense international conflict as
arouses the emotions of fear and hatred. (We know the psychology is that when you are afraid you hate; and when you hate you
are angry. In other words, the three emotions of fear, hatred, and
anger go together.)
I have two examples to put before you: one historical and the
other contemporary. The historical example is that of the use of
the atom bomb on Hiroshima and Nagasaki when Japan was
already, in effect, defeated—in other words, the altogether un-
necessary use of the atom bomb on Japan. And for the documentation of this there is a superb book by my former colleague,
Herbert Feis, *The Atom Bomb and the End of World War II*,
published by the Princeton University Press.
I say that in the winter of 1944 to 1945 Japan was already
defeated in effect. Here was an island nation, a crowded island
nation, that was absolutely dependent on the importation of food
from overseas, but so completely blockaded by the Allied navies
that not a crumb could be brought in. Just this, in itself, confronted the Japanese with the stark choice between surrender and
starvation. According to the official report of General George
Marshall, the American Chief of Staff, in July of 1945,

> [f]ighters from Iwo Jima swept the air over the Japa-
> nese islands, strafed Japanese dromes and communi-
> cations, and gave the superbombers freedom of opera-
> tion. The Third Fleet, augmented by British units,
> hammered Japan with its planes and guns, sailing
> boldly into Japanese coastal waters. The warships
> repeatedly and effectively shelled industries along the
> coast. These mighty attacks met little opposition.

More than this, Allied planes were flying with impunity at
housetop level all over the Japanese islands, bombing communications and what fragments of industry remained—in other
words, setting internal blockades so that food couldn't move.
And the fires they started, these planes flying over Japan, remained unextinguished because the Japanese fire-fighting apparatus was no longer functioning. Japan was a defeated nation and
clearly so.
Moreover, as we knew at the time, the Japanese by a succession of governmental reorganizations were trying to put them-

selves in a position to sue for peace and were begging Moscow, with which they had a neutrality pact, to use its good offices in order to obtain peace. (This is really tragic; it's almost a Shakespearean tragedy. The last place they should have gone was Moscow. Moscow did't want the war to end before it came in so it was not going to cooperate with the Japanese in bringing about a peace. The Japanese should have gone to the Nicaraguans or the Patagonians or anybody before they went to Moscow, but they went to Moscow.)

This was the situation as we knew it at the time. And yet, the civilian and military leaders of the United States and Britain were unanimous in seeing only one alternative to the use of the atom bomb, and also to the ardently solicited military intervention of the Soviet Union (which, of course, was the last thing they should have wished for). They saw only one alternative; that only alternative was an invasion of the Japanese home islands by Allied ground forces at an estimated cost of half a million or more Allied casualties. The assumption was that the Japanese were so fanatical that virtually every one of them would have to be dug out of his cellar across the length and breadth of Japan to achieve and enforce the unconditional surrender that unfortunately was required. (Nothing is so unfortunate as this requirement of "unconditional surrender," but I won't go into that. It was one of the reasons why one couldn't make a proper peace.)

No one, it appears, pointed out that even the most fanatical people have to eat in order to live. Even the most fanatical people have to eat in order to practice their fanaticism. The record shows that no Allied statesman, not one, questioned this view of the situation, and that, consequently, all the decision-makers welcomed the use of the atom bomb as salvation itself. Truman and Churchill were persuaded by their staffs and all their advisors that there was no acceptable alternative. (Read Truman's memoirs on this, read Churchill on it.) Everyone without exception agreed on this. I could refine this example in many ways, but this will do to illustrate what I have called "the dynamics of bureaucracy."

In the constant competition for place and influence in the Washington bureaucracy (and many of us beside myself have lived through this), victory went to those who were not so "softheaded" as to believe that the Japanese would ever give up. Therefore, as the only alternative to conquering Japan foot by foot, the Japanese men, women, and children would have to be subjected to indiscriminate atomization.

So much for my historical example of what I have called "the dynamics of bureaucracy." I've put it too crudely, but this can be discussed.

My contemporary example is that of the present race in nuclear armaments between the United States and the Soviet Union. This race, I maintain, makes as little sense as did the policy by which the war against Japan was brought to its appalling close—and here I really am being controversial. There will be a lot of people to disagree with me. But I repeat—this race makes as little sense as the policy by which the war against Japan was brought to its close. I can sum the matter up in a phrase by saying that *competition in overkill makes no sense.* If the Soviet Union can kill the United States ten times over, what difference does it make if the United States is able to kill the Soviet Union only five times over? The statistics no longer have their usual relevance.

I can make the same point by a simple simile which I've used before: if two men stand with loaded pistols to each other's heads, what difference does it make if the pistol of one is a .45 caliber and the pistol of the other is only a .22? What difference does it make? Either can kill the other just as dead by a single shot. What follows is that the man with the .22 doesn't need a .45 to make himself equal to the man who already has one. The two are already equal because either can kill the other by the pull of a trigger. I repeat, then, that competition in capacity for overkill makes no sense at all.

Let me put this now in operative rather than metaphoric terms. All the United States needs to deter aggression by the Soviet Union is the retaliatory capacity to inflict unacceptable damage on the Soviet Union. No matter how much greater the nuclear capacity of the Soviet Union may be, that's enough—the capacity to inflict unacceptable damage. And all the Soviet Union needs to deter aggression by the United States is the retaliatory capacity to inflict unacceptable damage on the United States, no matter how much greater the nuclear capacity of the United States may be. In the actual circumstances, to my mind, there is no problem in defining unacceptable damage, anymore than in the case of the two men with pistols at each other's heads. The capacity for unacceptable damage is the capacity which already exists—perhaps I exaggerate, but it exists in abundance—the capacity which already exists to destroy the other society as such. Any capacity beyond that is capacity for overkill, which makes no sense from the point of view of the country that has it. I put forward here a line of reasoning that no one in my personal experience, has been able to dispute. People disagree with it, but I've never really heard this particular argument disputed, nor do I know how one could do it.

If, then, the United States and the Soviet Union continue to pursue their arms race into the realm of overkill, the basic explanation must be in what I have called "the dynamics of bureaucracy." (I've been very close to this and I've seen it.)

As was the case with respect to Japan forty years ago, so today in the bureaucratic competition for place and influence, which must go on in Moscow as it does in Washington, victory goes to the hawks, victory goes to the hard-liners, victory goes to those who "are not so soft-headed as to underestimate the enemy."

I'm quite aware of the fact that the point I have made requires elaboration and qualification. I've made it in great simplicity, and in its simplicity it is open to all sorts of refinement and complexification. I've tried to give just the essence of the argument.

●　　●　　●

I've now raised questions that I hope will be discussed, and that will contribute to my own enlightenment. For one thing one has to ask where, in the hierarchy of bureaucratic government, the basic bureaucracy merges into the top political leadership, which may be presumed to have a certain independence of the basic bureaucracy.

In 1945, was the Secretary of War, Mr. Henry Stimson, simply a member of the bureaucracy, subject to its dynamics? Was General Marshall, the Chief of Staff, simply a member of the bureaucracy subject to its dynamics? Was President Truman? Is not a bureaucracy subject to direction from above? When I began to prepare these remarks, as I told Ken yesterday, I became terribly embarrassed because I began to think: I'm wrong. I should not confine this to bureaucracy. You know, it's only when you have to write or speak on a subject that you begin to think hard about it. This is true in my experience; it's the test of one's idle, daydreaming thoughts. It's wrong to confine this just to bureaucracy.

I remember vividly when the Truman Administration was replaced by the Eisenhower Administration in 1952—the beginning of McCarthyism and so on. What I called "the dynamics of bureaucracy" was exhibited in an extreme degree by the new administration that came in, and by no one in a more extreme degree than Mr. Dulles, the Secretary of State. I was in the office of the secretary of state at the time, and Mr. Dulles went to the utmost extremes. The effort then was to discredit the Roosevelt and Truman administrations as having been pro-Communist administrations, as having really been Communist. Acheson was the "Red Dean," you know, he was really said to be a Communist! So now you had an administration that was "realistic," it didn't engage in "wishful thinking." It didn't "underestimate the enemy," and so on. I sat by and watched Mr. Dulles—he had his great merits, I don't mean to attack him personally. Mr. Dulles promoted, as they all did, a most alarming picture of the state of the world, under the rubric of "realism." We all had the picture, in those days, of the Soviet Union under Stalin advancing to the conquest of the world on the basis of a "blueprint" and a "timetable"—those were the words we used—a "blueprint" and a "timetable" that had been left by Lenin. And people believed this, endorsed it, advanced it. You had the picture of this time-table, somewhere in a secret part of the Kremlin, where you'd have a list of dates, and down here would be "1950 Korea." And Lenin had written this and left it. The American people were told this kind of thing. Mr. Dulles was a ruthless person and in some sense would stop at nothing. I don't think he would murder his wife and children or anything, but short of murder, he'd stop at nothing to gain his ends. And Mr. Dulles, even in public speeches, quoted very alarming sayings of Lenin between quotation marks, that Lenin never made at all. Some of them I was so surprised at that I finally consulted the experts in Marxism and Leninism, and the students of the writings of Lenin, who said they had never heard of these statements—he never made them. Mr. Dulles would, presumably, invent them; he would compose them.

But, Mr. Dulles was not just a member of the bureaucracy, was he? So I'm talking about more than a bureaucracy. I'm talking about *the dynamics of consensus,* if you will. And one of the things than anybody who has lived in Washington knows is how it is almost impossible to go against a consensus. You can sit at the head of the table and you can believe one thing, but everybody else around the table says the opposite thing. Even a very strong-willed person can hardly assume the responsibility, when it *is* his responsibility, to go against this consensus.

Woodrow Wilson never had to face this. He didn't sit up at the head of a table confronted by all these people, by this consensus. This is especially true when you are dealing with a military situation and the people around the table are in uniform and you are a civilian. Mr. Truman was terribly vulnerable on this score because he had risen to the rank of being a captain in the Army in World War I, and consequently he had tremendous awe of the generals and admirals. (I understand this very well, because I hadn't risen above the rank of private in World War II in the U.S. Army and when I saw a major in the distance, which happened very rarely, I almost fell on my face. I was so in awe of a major.) And consequently, this going against the consensus, or going against the military—the President of the United States hardly dares do it when it is a matter of life and death for the nation.

I really am talking about more than bureaucracy, I am talking about the formation of foreign policy by a very wide consensus.

As regards the arms race, a relatively soft line prevailed in the Carter administration, and that's not so long ago. Does this contradict what I said when in the Carter administration apparently the hard-liners were *not* on top? But my tentative explanation of this, for discussion, is that the Carter administration represented the end of what we called the period of détente. I think, myself, that in historical perspective the historians writing the history books will talk about the First Cold War and the Second Cold War, and I've even seen this in print lately. There was the First Cold War from about 1947 to 1963, including the Cuban missile crisis. Then the United States and the Soviet Union came so close to hot war, or thought they did—I didn't think they did that they were alarmed and drew back. The "hot line" between Washington and Moscow was symbolic of the new relationship where they could cooperate, and there was a period of détente until about 1978, when the Soviet Union began deploying ABM systems, and this broke the understanding. We then had the development of "the Second Cold War," in the midst of which we are today. I would save my argument from being discredited by the experience of the Carter administration. The conflict was not that intense during the Carter administration but it was getting there. Of course the Carter administration tended to be discredited by the Reagan administration as the Truman administration had tended to be discredited by the Eisenhower administration.

This, of course, is an immense subject in itself and I think we all have some understanding of it though I would be hard put to analyze it. But there is also the immense element of the industrial vested interests in the arms race, which surely play a notable role today in keeping it up—the tremendous interest of industry and business and so on. I dare say this is as true in Moscow as it is in Washington, though it goes through other channels and takes other forms. Today this military–industrial relationship (which alarmed even Eisenhower, a military man) is beyond measuring, it is so immense. I'm not accusing people of wanting war or international conflict so that they can sell arms—like the sort of naive theory that developed after World War I that the arms manufacturers caused World War I. The people are sincere in believing that it is necessary to build all sorts of new and more destructive weapons. But their influence is immense, and I think if Woodrow Wilson, that strong-willed person, was President of the United States today and he wanted to stop the arms race, or he wanted to stop the American buildup, as strong a man as he was, I don't know whether he could do it against these immense vested interests. And that's a very pessimistic conclusion to come to because it suggests that there is no solution to the problem.

I've now presented a thesis that I hope may serve as a point of departure for a discussion. Thank you.

*Mr. Thompson:* Who would like to raise the first question and make any comment?

*Question:* That's very interesting and provocative and unquestionably in its main emphasis has validity. I want to know your view of the influence in all this of the new communications system—news by television, radio, and the kind of thinking this tends to generate—on the question of consensus, the influence of this perhaps in giving the president a way around the bureaucracy technically. I mean our President at the moment thinks he can go to the people and get almost anything he wants, and this is a whole new element.

*Mr. Halle:* It would take me about twenty-four hours of hard thought to give you an intelligent, meaningful answer to what you ask. It is an awfully good question. I would say immediately that this democratic element enlarges tremendously the "mass"—I'll use the metaphor of the physicist—the mass of consensus, the gravitational mass of consensus, the inertial mass of consensus. It is tremendously increased by this, and in a sense the government controls this consensus.

When the Eisenhower administration came in and Dulles took this line, he formed public opinion, did he not? Maybe he formed a public opinion that was already forming because the American people were panic stricken. The Korean War and the loss of China, as it was called, panicked Americans. They were in a state of great alarm. Dulles played to this. He increased the alarm, if anything, by this "blueprint" and the "timetable" of Lenin's—this damn nonsense. So you had the consensus generating and then intensifying itself on a much wider scale because we are a country in which public opinion prevails.

The situation would be different in the Soviet Union, but perhaps not in a radical way. The Soviet Union controls its public opinion, and its public opinion, I take it, is sort of passive. It believes in a rather cynical way. But by and large, this cynicism is just the icing on the cake; it's a superficial thing. Their view of the world is the view of the world, I believe, as presented by the government, and it increases the gravitational mass of the consensus.

*Question:* Just one follow-up comment to that. Mass—agreed, inertia—I'm not sure. It can move faster now than it ever could.

*Mr. Halle:* You haven't been reading Einstein. Inertia and gravitational mass are the same thing.

*Mr. Thompson:* Our next question should be asked by our physicist.

*Question:* It certainly is extremely interesting what you have to say. The arms race is certainly a complicated thing, it is something of great current interest. Of course this business of the bullet at the head is not a fully accurate analogy. Some people at least might say it's a bullet at a distance and therefore you may require a second shot, just as our weapons are at a distance, and it is a question of knocking out the retaliatory capability of the enemy. You'd probably lump that into the question of further and deeper explanation.

*Mr. Halle:* I wouldn't go to great lengths to defend what was simply a metaphor.

*Question:* No, I understand.

*Mr. Halle:* But I do have an opinion, on the basis of such knowledge as I have today. Of course these things are never finally judged until the test of battle, which I hope will never happen. Both countries have their nuclear retaliatory capacity so well defended that they would have enough left after a first strike to destroy the other country. I believe this to be true. So that would make the analogy good. I do believe that either could kill the other at one shot but, as I say, this is metaphoric. It would be subject to the opinion of those more informed than I am.

*Question:* It does involve technical questions.

*Mr. Halle:* I don't regard it as particularly technical. I have discussed this with people inside the government who have access to all the information, who are in the arms-control business. They are responsible people and they say, "What do you mean by unacceptable damage?" I say, off the top of my head: "The ability to destroy the six principal Soviet cities overnight." This is just an arbitrary definition. The ability to destroy the society means that the society is dead the next day. You don't have a Communist Soviet Union, you don't have a Jeffersonian United States, you just have chaos and no government. Society is fragmented. And I think this would happen—or the chances of its happening are so great that it would be a deterrent. And this probability is what counts; it's not the knowledge that it would *not* happen.

I could go farther today—perhaps I shouldn't add this new thing. I think nobody has appreciated yet the radical impact of the discovery of the probability of "nuclear winter." We all have read about the "nuclear winter." It has been presented as probable. The "nuclear winter" means that probably the consequence of a first strike that was large enough to be a disarming strike—and of course this would have to be a very large strike—would mean the darkening of the skies over the Northern Hemisphere and beyond the Northern Hemisphere into the Southern Hemisphere—the darkening of the skies, the lowering of the temperature to a degree where food could no longer be grown, resulting in mass starvation by billions in the Northern and even the Southern Hemisphere. This would be a probability; this would mean the end of these societies—mass starvation, total chaos. I welcome this enormously because, of course, the decision on a first strike would be a collective decision. (The President of the United States does not have a button on his bedside table.) If you just imagine a meeting in the White House, or imagine a meeting in the Kremlin—I make no distinction—of people to consider launching a first strike when the consequences might be the end of our own society—the outcome would probably be this. Under the circumstances they really could not do it. They might be as wicked as you please. Even here in Charlottesville, I make no distinction between Jeffersonians and Leninists when it comes to this. They could not do it. It would be the probable defeat of everything they had ever stood for.

*Question:* Sir, have you discussed these matters lately with your two former colleagues, George Kennan and Paul Nitze, who seem to have somewhat opposing views on it?

*Mr. Halle:* That's right. I really don't agree with George Kennan. And I don't agree with Paul Nitze—although I have the greatest respect for both men. We've argued about these things. The arguments are the kind of arguments that are open-ended, they never come to a conclusion. I always think if we had a week to walk around the mountains together, perhaps we'd come to an agreed conclusion.

*Question:* You spoke of the dynamics of the bureaucracy and its impact on secretaries and presidents, and then you also mentioned how the bureaucracy has various ways of influencing public opinion, and obviously it's an interactive system. How much thought have you given to the intricacies of how well the bureaucracy in turn reflects public consensus? Obviously the communication goes both ways. To what extent is it responsible? One sometimes has the impression that the bureaucracy is totally oblivious to public opinion, and sometimes it is keenly attuned to it and shifts almost too quickly. I wonder if you have explored that.

*Mr. Halle:* I can't give you a very profound answer on that. One of the things that I've often noticed is that intellectuals think that their own opinion is public opinion. It's an extraordinary phenomenon.

I believe—though I'm very shaky on this and I may be wrong—there is a general belief that the American public was very much against the Vietnam War. I think it was the intellectuals who were very much against it. I think, perhaps, if one had taken a poll of the entire population of the United States, one would have found a majority in favor of the Vietnam War, rather than opposed to it.

*Comment:* Any president who ran in 1964 on pulling out of the Vietnam War wouldn't have gotten twenty percent of the votes.

*Mr. Halle:* In other words—among the American public generally. Now you have to modify this again by saying a lot of this public opinion, if you took this vote, is an inert public opinion. The farmer behind his plow in Kansas or Iowa, if you asked him he'd say, "Yes, we ought to beat these Commies. We ought to stay until we have victory" or something like that. But he doesn't carry much weight, whereas an intellectual who is writing for the newpapers and magazines on the opposite side—that represents influential public opinion. It represents, shall we say, active public opinion.

*Question:* Let me throw out a crude theory on this relationship between consensus, public opinion and bureaucratic power. It seems to me that bureaucracy can thwart the president or shape what the president does primarily when the bureaucracy has the latent power to appeal to a segment of public opinion that will be responsive to it and that will act differently. It seems in public opinion you have two very strong tendencies. In a period of uncertainty, war being uncertainty, the public tends to gravitate very strongly toward the person who wants to be strong, firm, and tough with the Russians. And when you are competing for a policy decision in which strong, tough, and firm might deviate from some alternative that would be described, critically perhaps, as prudent, the chips are on the side of the strong and firm crowd.

When we are in a period that is not uncertain, the strong public tendency in this country, still latent and still having expression when things are not uncertain, is to be complacent. Then you get a bureaucracy which seeks to excite or to get defense appropriations or whatever you will of that nature. It has a tough time and other voices are heard, maybe not any wiser. You had this, for instance, in the very early 1970s as a reaction to Vietnam. There is no question that the quality of analysis of our defense needs, however one cuts the cake, in the early seventies just didn't have much effect on it. Congress wasn't going to appropriate money for defense in the first five years of the seventies. I think those, if you will, are the two sorts of general tendencies in the public, and that the reflections of that sentiment in the bureaucracy determines whether the president has problems with the bureaucracy shaping him or vice versa.

*Mr. Halle:* This is the answer I would have given you if I had known as much.

*Question:* It's rather strange that we do have this massive confrontation but it's rather difficult to put your finger any place on the face of the earth where there is a definite threat compared say, to Hitler's threat to Europe in the 1930s. We knew exactly where the threat was then because it was always backed by a vast massing of armies along borders. There is no such thing like that today, and yet we have these global fears. That's what I call a rather strange phenomenon.

You answered the question earlier in your talk when you talked about the development of these enormous fears in the days of Truman which became the common wisdom. That's what I would refer to, the sudden development of these massive fears which really don't have any basis in fact but they simply arise and are accepted and repeated over and over again, embodied in such things as the Truman Doctrine and so on. This thing keeps moving on and on and on which creates massive fears to sustain the Cold War in the absence of any definite threat that you can point your finger to. And in a sense that's a theme I'm developing.

*Mr. Halle:* I do, myself, think that there *is* a threat. There is a very real threat. I think there is a long-term and not very specific threat. It is that the continuation of the Russian empire historically has been an expanding phenomenon, beginning with the Kiev state in the ninth century. This is a great power expanding and pushing against its frontiers for reasons that I won't go into. In a word, it has to be "contained."

*Mr. Graebner:* I never deny that. In fact, I make it very clear that there is this constant pressure on the peripheries.

*Mr. Halle:* May I say, perhaps shocking some of you, that the United States, too, has to be contained; any great power has to be contained. In 1950, when the Eisenhower administration came in, it came in on a program, not of containing the Soviet Union but of liberating the satellite countries. If the Soviet Union had been weak enough, we would have liberated the satellites. I think so. In other words, I'm a great believer in the balance of power. You've got to have the balance, and just as the Soviet Union has to be balanced, so the United States has to be balanced. It's not a case of wickedness or anything like that, but powers tend to expand. They push out against each other, and the only way we can get peace is a balance of power. If the Soviet Union is not balanced and if the United States is not balanced, they are going to have an upset leading to war.

*Question:* But don't you have to have a threat in the sense that we've never had it before, speaking of threats? Threat to what? You don't talk about threats unless you talk about what is threatened. And presumably, it is the threat to your security. And in the modern age of nuclear arms, the capacity to defend yourself with any kind of armaments doesn't exist as long as the other side has nuclear power. You cannot take care of your own security by your own devices, and that is threatening in the extreme. Unless you go to some kind of world government you have no provision for your national security.

*Mr. Halle:* There are two statements that you make: one is that there is no *defense*. I would agree with this. The other is that you can't provide for your own security, and I would disagree with this because what has taken the place of defense is *deterrence*.

*Question:* Yes, but that's to abdicate the responsibility. The concept of security was that you provided to deter the other side; if deterrence failed then you defeated whoever attacked you in war. That last option in the nuclear age is no longer there. Our security rests on what the people in Moscow decide to do and there's nothing we can do that will protect our security, and the same thing is true of them.

*Mr. Halle:* We can deter them.

*Question:* Deter them is making them think they don't want to do it.

*Mr. Halle:* That's right.

*Question:* We don't have control over what they think. That's what I'm saying.

*Mr. Halle:* The consequences to them would be suicidal.

*Question:* Oh, I understand deterrence, but deterrence depends on whether they decide to do it, not on what we do ultimately.

*Mr. Halle:* But their decision is subject to influence.

*Question:* That is a different thing than providing for your security.

*Question:* Anything that I might say simply underscores the basic thesis of your whole talk. Your reference to Woodrow Wilson was simply a reminder of how personal American diplomacy was from the beginning through the time of Wilson, with John Quincy Adams and Seward and these men operating so magnificently as individuals. And there is not any record that they talked to anyone except themselves in developing brilliant policies. I think the difference also is in the quotability of those early statements as opposed to the present; nothing is very quotable any more. But Seward and Wilson are quotable because there is a brilliance in their writings.

You mentioned two episodes to suggest this bureaucratic momentum: one was the decision to use the atomic bomb in 1945 and the other one being the more recent development of the arms race. I would simply suggest that you've got a marvelous one between the two in the 1950s in the enormous amount of bureaucratic in fighting between Eisenhower and the Washington bureaucracy on the development of atomic weaponry, the beginnings of overkill. By the time you get to the end of the decade we have allegedly 18,000 nuclear warheads aimed at 2,500 Soviet targets, some them overlaid so heavily that some targets could be hit seventeen times over with nuclear weapons. That's where we have gotten, and so in the context of that you can see what Eisenhower is saying in his great farewell address to the American people, "I had five stars and I couldn't control them. What's a poor civilian president going to do?"

So the question I want to raise is simply this: to what extent do you think the bureaucracy reflects the views of those above it?

*Mr. Halle:* The bosses above?

*Question:* Yes. In other words, the bureaucracy is moving in a Cold War direction under Eisenhower. But remember Eisenhower and Dulles are also reflecting such views at the top. Today you get the same thing; that is, these views are being reflected at the top. I wondered to what extent you feel that the bureaucracy, as it develops and maintains rather hard-line approaches, is reflecting the views of the leaders at the top, and to what extent shifting views at the top might have an impact on the bureaucracy?

*Mr. Halle:* This is something that I have not thought out and I can see the complexities of it. There are, of course, interactions. Anybody who has lived in a bureaucracy knows that you tend to agree with the boss. When a new man comes in with new opinions everybody in the bureaucracy immediately under him, those who are dependent on him, share his opinions. We've all had the experience in a bureaucracy. We sit around the table and the boss says, "Well, here is the question; this is my opinion, what is your opinion?" Anybody with any sense, and Dean Acheson had this kind of sense, poses the question and waits to give his own opinion until everybody else has spoken. But this is only one of many interactions, and instead of trying to answer your question, I would just flounder unless I had been able to think more about it.

*Mr. Thompson:* I wonder what you'd say about the counter-thesis. In a way you've turned conventional political and diplomatic analysis on its head. The traditional view has been that the bureaucracy was the stabilizing force; it was the balance wheel. According to this view, you always had moderate people in government but the last two administrations have tended to be ideological administrations. Some of the top military and naval people who are part of the bureaucracy are much more critical of the current management and administration of the Defense Department and defense policy than any outside analyst. So the opposite view has been, whether it be in Britain or in this country, that the so-called permanent government has been a stabilizing force. When President Reagan came in, he issued an order (Richard Allen and others were supposed to have prepared it) that everybody from the rank of assistant secretary, including the assistant secretary, with presidential appointments should clear their desks by the next day. It was not the political transition team that urged the order be changed but Al Haig and the incoming State Department group who asked for an exception for

seven or eight people and later some more to continue simply to
do the business of the State Department.

Les Gelb, when he spoke here, said that one of the things he
thought in retrospect was bad in the Carter administration was
that people who came in on the transition team all had the same
political ideology and point of view. It took time and it took
listening to the messengers who brought the message nobody
wanted to hear from within the bureaucracy before they changed.
So that's the opposite view, or is it an opposite view? Is it at odds
with your view or not?

*Mr. Halle:* No, I think this is true. There are all sorts of forces
in dynamic relations, and there are opposing forces, counter-
forces. Anybody who like me and others have lived for years in
the bureaucracy knows how the bureaucracy can defeat the
leadership if they don't agree. If you are the leader and a strong
man like Woodrow Wilson, you try to get the bureaucracy to go
along the path that it is not disposed to go because bureaucracy
can defeat you. These are all forces.

There are all sorts of tricks we bureaucrats played. When
General Marshall became secretary of state he was appalled by
all the paper that came to him to read beyond his or anybody's
capacity. And so he issued an order, military fashion, that no
memorandum should be more than a page long, one typewritten
page. So we, down in the bowels of the bureaucracy, would get a
message that Secretary Marshall wanted a memorandum giving
him a report on the situation in Alaska, as related to the situation
in Siam, as related to the plight of the whales in the Antarctic
Ocean, as related to the consequences of a war with Japan, and so
on. We had to give it in a page. So we would give it in half a page,
and then we would wait until he came back and said, "Well, I
need more than that." Then we would give him three pages. The
bureaucracy can always defeat leaders. So there are all these
forces. There is the force of the leadership on the bureaucracy,
which is, of course, very effective and tremendous. There is also
a counterforce. All these things exist. It's a complex situation.

*Mr. Thompson:* I thought the most compelling example, even
more so than the two you gave this morning, was "the walk in the

woods" example. I don't know if you would be willing to cite that.

*Mr. Halle:* I understand Ken to be referring, now, to the recent negotiations that went on in Geneva for a couple of years between the American delegation under Paul Nitze and the Soviet delegation under Yuli Kvitsinsky in an effort which came to nothing, to reach agreement on limiting the deployment of inter-mediate-range nuclear arms in Europe. Nitze and Kvitsinsky were both what we call "hawks" on their respective opposed sides. Neither would be disposed to give anything away in terms of his side's position. They did not reach agreement, even be-tween themselves as individuals, on the terms of a settlement. But they did, at one point, reach agreement on submitting to their respective governments in Washington and Moscow a single set of proposals for consideration by those governments. The set of proposals was jointly formulated in an all-day walk that just the two of them took along the forested slopes of the Jura mountains near Geneva. This was the now famous "walk in the woods" to which Ken refers. As we all know, both governments (both bureaucracies, I would say) immediately rejected the package of proposals that emerged from that talk.

My own purely personal opinion as an onlooker in Geneva is that if ultimate agreement on the terms of a settlement of the race with respect to intermediate arms had depended only on those two opposed hawks, Nitze and Kvitzinsky, it would have been reached. It would have been posssible, I myself think, for the two men to reach agreement where it was impossible for the two bureaucracies to reach agreement because of what I have called "the dynamics of bureaucracy."

In this context, I recall nostalgically what Talleyrand, Met-ternich, Castlereagh, and the rest were able to accomplish in 1815 because they did not have great bureaucracies to which they were bound. What they were able to accomplish, in the absence of such bureaucracies, was a century of relative peace.

*Mr. Thompson:* We thank Louis Halle for challenging us to think more deeply about "the dynamics of bureaucracy."

PART TWO

# Complex
# Discourse in
# National Security
# Policy-making

# Staffing the White House for Foreign Policy: Some Dilemmas*
## I. M. DESTLER

I. M. Destler received his Master of Public Affairs and Ph.D. from the Woodrow Wilson School at Princeton University. He did his undergraduate work at Harvard. He is currently a senior fellow of the Institute of International Economics in Washington. Not long ago, he was a senior associate and project director of the Carnegie Endowment for International Peace and a senior fellow at the Brookings Institution.

He has published widely in both the foreign policy field and in the international economic policy field. He was a consultant on the economic aspects of foreign policy and is the leading analyst of an Office of Management and Budget study of the organization of the government for foreign policy-making. He has written a series of books on foreign policy, the most recent with Gelb and Lake being *Our Own Worst Enemy,* which treats the topic of this essay. He also has written a well-known book, *Presidents, Bureaucrats, and Foreign Policy* which has been used by those of us who teach international relations because it deals with the organization of the government for foreign policy-making. The present topic is staffing the White House for foreign policy. He approaches the topic as one of the leading figures in the field of international relations, economic policy making and the public administration aspects of foreign policy problems.

*Dr. Destler:* Thank you very much, Ken. It's a pleasure to be here. As you were kindly reciting from memory, and I must say accurately, my various titles, I was thinking of a more succinct introduction I got a couple of years ago at a talk in which the introducer said that I had "thought in several tanks."

*Presented at the Miller Center on September 26, 1985.

*Mr. Thompson:* He has also taught at several universities such as Princeton and the School for Advanced International Studies. He will be teaching in the spring of 1986 at the International University of Tokyo, and next summer at the Salzburg Seminar. In short, he's not completely "tanked."

*Dr. Destler:* I think we'll move away from this metaphor fairly quickly. Ken has asked me to think out loud for a few minutes about the subject of presidential foreign policy staffing, to share some of the historical and analytic perspective that I've developed on the problem. I'll talk mostly about the policy sphere for which there has been most of the foreign policy staffing in the White House, that is, national security policy. Only at the end will I talk a little bit about the staffing—or, as often as not, the lack of it or the inadequacy of it—for international economic policy questions.

As most of you know, there has been some explicit staffing in the White House for foreign policy since the creation of a National Security Council (NSC) by the National Security Act of 1947. So we are now talking about institutions that are getting very close to forty years old. The staffing of foreign policy has always been formally attached to the National Security Council, a Cabinet level committee. In practice, however, it has more often than not, not served the Council *per se* as much as it has served the president.

I think it is useful historically to think about foreign policy staffing in the White House as going through three stages. I want to lay out these stages, and then make some generalizations about each. Those of you who have close experience in one of these or a portion thereof can offer the necessary correctives in the discussion period thereafter.

I'll divide the stages first by presidents. The first stage was basically under Truman and Eisenhower, the period up to the Eisenhower-Kennedy transition. The second stage of White House foreign policy staffing was in the Kennedy-Johnson period. You can date the end of this period as either the Johnson-Nixon transition, or, as I would tend to do it, maybe a year or two after that. The third stage continued from around 1970 to the present. Looking at these various stages, we can ask certain questions about the type of staffing, what staff members saw their job as being, and what they did.

One question is what types of individuals worked in the White House on foreign policy. Basically, during the first stage, the Truman-Eisenhower stage, you had a careerist staff; you had people who were civil servants or foreign service officers or occasionally military officers, but the basic pattern was civil service. There was continuity; the notion was that there would be an ongoing staff from administration to administration, similar to the then Bureau of the Budget, now the Office of Management and Budget.

Another question is the partisan orientations of a staff. Basically, I would characterize the NSC staff in the Truman-Eisenhower years as what you would expect from a careerist, civil service group. They were nonpartisan, except for the top person, then called Executive Secretary, later Special Assistant to the President, who was of course a presidential appointee.

Looking at policy orientation, it seems to me you had staff aides who were basically centrist. They were part of the very broad foreign policy consensus about the desirability of U. S. activism in the world. They differed in their views on certain issues and in their emphasis, but they were similar in orientation. They worked not for the president directly but for the interagency process, in which an effort was made to do relatively long-range planning, to establish priorities, to establish policy goals and reach interagency agreement on them. That was essentially their goal. Their operational role was in the facilitation of long-range planning. Those who dislike the process, particularly in the Eisenhower administration, called it a cumbersome papermill, arguing that the paper processing led to unreal decisions. Those who liked it said that it was a thorough and systematic means of drawing issues and giving them careful analytical attention.

Finally, the staff and its chief clearly saw themselves as subordinate to the Cabinet level. If you look at the public profile, we are talking basically about an anonymous staff. There were some exceptions: Bobby Cutler, Eisenhower's special assistant, did some public speaking and wrote an article for *Foreign Affairs*. But by and large the staff was relatively low profile.

Let me turn to the second stage. Whereas the staff in the

earlier period had been a careerist staff with personnel continuing on from administration to administration, in the Kennedy and Johnson administrations turnover rather than continuity became the norm. You had the coming in of what Dick Neustadt and others labeled the "in and outers," people who didn't necessarily have government service as their primary career.

Secondly, it follows that whereas the first group could be considered nonpartisan, this group was more "administration identified." McGeorge Bundy may have been a Republican—he was a Republican through the Kennedy and at least some of the Johnson administration—but there was no question but that he had come in to serve the president, or those particular presidents; and it wasn't assumed that if the other party took power he or his chief subordinates would stay on.

The policy orientation was still basically, I would argue, centrist. People might give some argument about this; there were some differences of emphasis between the Eisenhower and Kennedy administrations, but people were still operating, I think, within a broad consensus.

Next, and this was an important change, instead of serving the NSC process, the White House NSC staff was now serving the president. They were serving him personally, supporting his personal engagement. Eisenhower, in fact, had a different staff support person outside of the National Security Council staff to serve his personal needs and handle his personal business on foreign policy. For Kennedy, the NSC staff, the official and foreign policy staff, became the staff that served the president himself. It followed that the staff's role changed, particularly when a president was very much involved in action and wanted to be in the center of action, wanted to make day-to-day decisions himself, as Kennedy and Johnson did. The job changed from formal planning to facilitating daily foreign policy decisions and actions.

If in the earlier period the chief of staff was clearly subordinated to the Cabinet, now you had kind of a coexistence. Bundy and his successor Rostow were still somewhat subordinated to the Secretaries of State and Defense in form, but they were beginning to be near coequals; and on some issues, they might be predominant. This was particularly true for Bundy. They were no longer anonymous; they were what I would call semi-visible.

They didn't get their names in the *New York Times* nearly as much as some of their successors, but they were known and certainly many newspaper articles began to appear about the Bundy staff supplanting the secretary of state, taking over foreign policy from the White House, and so forth.

Then, under Nixon we had another transition which I think has set the pattern which has existed to the present day. The Kennedy emphasis on "in and outers" was continued. When I say "in and outers" I don't mean all the people came from outside the government. They included in any given time, staff members who were career or semi-career government officials chosen for this assignment because of their compatibility with other people already on the White House foreign policy staff. So they would not have an institutional identity separate from the administration: they would come in for limited tours. The staff also got much larger during this period: from the ten to twenty professionals who worked on policy in the Kennedy-Johnson period it grew to thirty or fifty thereafter. It became, I would argue, partisan. I should clarify what I mean by this; I don't mean that people in the foreign policy staff ever since Nixon necessarily have thought of themselves in terms of playing a partisan-political role primarily. In fact, when Henry Kissinger was asked to take the job of national security assistant under Nixon, he replaced almost all of the Johnson holdovers, but he brought in people who were very much like them with very much the same sort of range of views, basically centrist people. But then Vietnam began to have an increasingly polarizing effect; some of the people on that staff left; some of them joined the public critics of Vietnam policy, and then the Muskie and McGovern campaigns. There began to be more of a political loyalty test, not necessarily explicit, but a norm of concern that people on the staff be politically loyal in a partisan sense.

Polarization developed among the foreign policy expert community in the United States. Presidencies began to reflect this polarization: Carter rejected, or seemed to reject, many of the foreign policy premises of previous administrations, and Reagan has rejected even more of the Carter policy premises.

The staff tended to reflect this partisan polarization. Sometimes they did more than reflect it; sometimes they energized and embodied it even more than the presidents themselves. Thus, the staff has tended to move from being centrist in policy orientation to being more polarized.

The staff still serves the president, and still focuses primarily on day-to-day operational issues. The power and influence of the national security assistant now tends to more than equal that of the Cabinet members. Kissinger was the most notable and dramatic example of this. He was predominant in a way that no foreign policy official has been since World War II, with the possible exception of Dean Acheson. Brzezinski achieved a considerable predominance late in the Carter administration. Judge Clark was, I think by most assessments, the prime mover of Reagan administration foreign policy in 1983, until he left to become the secretary of the interior. Robert McFarlane, the current incumbent, would not be so characterized to date, but he certainly is becoming a more important and more powerful figure as his tenure continues.

Finally we have the question of the public profile. We have a movement toward very substantial visibility. Again this has fluctuated somewhat among individuals. Under President Ford, Brent Scowcroft did the job very well, in much more the old-fashioned way of a staff facilitator, a presenter of options to the President. But the normal pattern has been for considerable publicity.

I don't want to talk too much longer because I want to encourage questions. What are some of the net results of the trends which I've tried to capsulize? One is that there is a tendency now to emphasize change in policy over continuity, whereas the earlier NSC staffing was designed to provide continuity, to provide thorough integration of policy. There is now greater polarity, greater change, greater turnover, greater action orientation, an emphasis on policy changes, differentiating this President from the previous one.

Now these changes owe much to changes in our broader society, as it addresses the world and as it perceives world changes. My co-authors, Les Gelb and Tony Lake, and I have tried to address these in our book *Our Own Worst Enemy*. These staff changes also owe a great deal to presidential desire for policy initiative: presidents don't necessarily want a smoothly functioning, well integrated system because they want action; they may not be aware of or sensitive to the costs of a lack of coordination.

They are often looking for areas where they as individuals can make a mark and for people who will be able to support them in making this mark.

The difference is also reflected, it seems to me, in how presidential transitions have changed. For its time the Eisenhower-Kennedy transition looked pretty radical, at least to the Eisenhower NSC people who were pushed out and whose system was denounced as ineffective and meaningless by the Kennedy people. Ironically, that transition was symbolized by two men who had in a sense a lot of personal attachment to continuity. I'm thinking first of McGeorge Bundy who was a very assertive and aggressive national security assistant yet recognized the need to keep the government together. He very often went out of his way to be sure that the Secretary of State's prerogatives were respected, and, the records suggest, leaned against Kennedy's free-wheeling style to try to keep a sense of process which would tend to constrain people and keep them together.

Dick Neustadt, Kennedy's private transition adviser, also played an interesting role. Neustadt was very much a champion of Kennedy and very much a critic of Eisenhower; he also had a sense of government as institution, the historic roots of various government entities. He was inclined to look backward as well as forward and argued for the need to know and be sensitive to how government had worked.

We've moved a long way since then. The large lists of transition aides in both the Ford-Carter and the Carter-Reagan transitions reflect the greater polarization in the foreign policy expert community. We have people who are visibly identified with the new administration and whose priority is likely to be changing the policy which any president will have, but without a priority to process comparable to the one we had in earlier transitions. Richard Allen, the first Reagan national security assistant, is an example of this. Allen's White House experience was not very successful because he was not really that effective as an internal government man. He was much more effective as an organizer of conservative opinion and adviser to presidential candidates.

This highlights an anomaly. The White House staff agencies are crucial to keeping some sort of continuous orderly government structure, but they have now become the most fluid, the places where it is easist to change, where appointments tend to be less constrained than the senior appointments in the departments. Appointees don't have to be confirmed by the Senate; each president is presumed to have greater latitude and his aides are presumed to have greater latitude. White House staffs tend to be the places where the young activists are more likely to go. So you get greater fluidity in the institution where you would like to have some continuity.

Let me close with a few words about foreign economic policy staff. For national security, one of the problems has been the tendency of the staff to become too policy dominant, taking over policies rather than coordinating and facilitating them. You certainly don't have that problem in White House international economic policy staffing. It is often difficult to figure out where it is; you don't have a clear pattern. There are some periods like the Kennedy and Johnson administrations when you had a small staff attached to a deputy national security assistant who was in charge of coordinating international economic issues. That was a useful device. In the Ford administration and to some degree in the Nixon administration, people responsible for economic policy staffing handled the international dimension of economic policy. In both cases it was difficult to link national security to domestic and economic policy in making decisions.

It is often argued that there should be an analogue to the National Security Council, an International Economic Policy Council. In fact, some of you will remember that we had one in the Nixon and Ford administrations, from 1971 to 1977. But I think this prescription, though well intended, basically gets the problem backwards. It reverses cause and effect. The idea is that such a staff could look at a policy—for example, Jimmy Carter's grain embargo—before a decision was made. They could make calculations about the effect on world grain markets, effects on American farmers, etc. Similarly, when the president was developing an economic program somebody might say, "Wait a minute, what's going to happen to the dollar if you cut taxes, and how is that going to affect the economic balance?" Logically, this would be a good idea.

The big problem has been that that hasn't been the way presidents have thought of issues, and it hasn't been the way that the political system has tended to put these issues to presidents.

Issues in the international economic area come to presidents mainly either as foreign policy issues or as domestic economic issues. So you always have a staff channel for foreign policy and some sort of advisory network, although it may not be a single staff, coordinating economic policy questions. General international economic questions tend to be an orphan in this process. Trade is a partial exception here because there is a special White House coordinating institution.

I argued in a book I wrote at Brookings several years ago that unless international economic policy is given real presidential priority, meaning that presidential involvement in international economic issues becomes comparable to what it has been in foreign policy and general economic policy, the problem of government malcoordination can't be solved by creating a new staff. Staffs get their primary leverage from links to the business of the president.

Therefore, if you want to improve coordination you are better off with second best solutions. If you have a good national security staff operation going in a particular administration, attach an international economic deputy to that staff, and try to establish links between the national security and domestic economic policy-makers. If you have a good economic policy coordinating staff, then perhaps you would prefer to attach the international economic deputy to that side. That's where I come out on that subject.

*Mr. Thompson:* Dwayne Andreas, who chaired President Reagan's Foreign Economic Commission and is an associate of the Miller Center, presented the opposite point of view when he spoke here a few months ago. He argued that subsidies, dumping and unfair trade practices by other nations, had become so damaging, that we needed an economic security council. Do you have any thoughts on that?

*Dr. Destler:* Assuming that his premise is valid, I would argue that one of the reasons that subsidies and dumping have become so prominent politically is that we have a huge trade deficit whose causes mainly lie elsewhere. But assuming he is right, that it is looming large politically and that something needs to be done, I'm not certain that current staffing arrangements aren't reasonably adequate to deal with the problem. You do have some split in responsibility between the president's trade representative and the secretary of commerce. This should be corrected. I would argue for reversing the Reagan administration's department of trade proposal, by moving all or most of Commerce's trade operations from that Department to a unit under the trade representative's office. This should provide somewhat greater coherence. It might logically lend also, I think, to elimination of the Commerce Department.

However, our law in many of these areas is designed to limit presidential flexibility. If you deal with subsidies, the countervailing duty law states that there are certain objective measures that are supposed to be applied in a quantitative way and that the president is not supposed to interfere with that process. It is to be done by the staff of the Commerce Department, and the secretary of commerce is to make the final decision. Now there are other authorities that the president does have that are more flexible in trade. But if one argues we ought to have a more assertive trade policy in a more centralized institution, this would require that we change some of the laws that had been designed to limit presidential flexibility.

*Mr. Thompson:* Who'd like to ask the first question?

*Question:* I have a question about the relationship between Don Regan and President Reagan in the White House, and Mr. McFarlane. In his own quiet way, McFarlane may be an effective fighter. I wonder how you would rate this current system in terms of effectiveness.

*Dr. Destler:* That's a good question. Let me divide it into two parts. First, one thing I have focused on a lot in my previous analyses and writings is the relationships among the senior people. It seems to me that if you look at the national security side, specifically the relationship between the national security assistant and the Secretary of State, it's pretty good right now. McFarlane and Shultz seem to have worked out a compatible division of roles. They frequently work together on issues. McFarlane, although he is prominent publicly and does speak on the record on policy issues, does not do so in a way in which he appears to be an aspiring Secretary of State. Shultz has not contested his ability to coordinate, and I think Shultz has asserted himself and shown that he can be the dominant or the most influential foreign policy figure. One of his problems is that key issues, like arms control and Soviet relations, are on policy subjects with which he is not completely comfortable, and that, I think, limits his assertiveness. But if you look at the relationship between the National Security Council staff and the State Department, which I had written critically about during the Carter administration and the Nixon administration, those problems of destructive competition do not exist to the same degree in the current Reagan administration. That assessment is independent of what my views would be on the policy substance that is coming out.

I have more serious reservations on the new chief of staff arrangement. My sense is that Donald Regan is a strong and feared internal manager, which means that people inside the system, including Cabinet members, tend to defer to him. However, he doesn't have a similar reputation in the broader community or with the Congress, and he is not well regarded in terms of his political sensitivities. So, therefore, the danger is that in the short run he becomes more powerful internally, but isn't being sufficiently responsive externally. McFarlane has a separate channel to the President, but most of the domestic people don't; so the administrative capacity for adjustment is limited and the situation tends to get worse. I think one of the reasons the buildup of congressional concern and action on trade this spring and summer went on longer than it should have, without a serious administration response, was that Don Regan didn't take it seriously enough. His antenna weren't at all good on this issue, and other people who had a better sense of things didn't have regular access to the President.

To sum up then, I would say that in terms of relationships and roles the McFarlane-Shultz connection looks pretty good, but Regan's role as Chief of Staff is troubling.

*Question:* I'd like to go back a minute to this evolution of the presidential staff from the old traditional, facilitating, coordinating sort of role through to the more publicized or political sort of role you described. The aspect of that that interests me most is this: why did it all happen? That is to say, is there something in world conditions, or in American society, or in political life that brought this about? What is your view as to the fundamental underlying cause of that shift over a period of thirty or forty years?

*Dr. Destler:* I think there are several causes. I would point more to factors within the United States than to world conditions. I would mention a couple: one is that we have an independent presidency, unlike most governments where the executive and legislature are intertwined. This is often emphasized on the congressional side of our government: we have a more independent Congress, the president can't deliver Congress. But it's also true that our executive branch is more independent. The president has more leeway in terms of staffing. One explanation for the change in staffing is simply the gradual realization of the potential that all presidents and their aides have had to bring in more people to support their short-term objectives on a range of issues. It happened only gradually because there were traditional norms about the primacy of the departments and about who should be involved in foreign policy. These tended to limit this phenomenon in the earlier period.

Another general explanation has to do with the broader opening up of American politics in the post-war period, and the opening up of the foreign policy community as a part of that. In general, politics has become a more free-wheeling entrepreneurial activity. In foreign policy, in the immediate post-war period, there was a relatively limited number of foreign policy specialists, who were finally succeeding in their mission of making the United States an active and creative presence in the world. As more international affairs education became available, this group expanded. After Vietnam caused some to ask fundamental questions about the premise of past policy, but didn't have that effect on others, there was a polarization. This meant that different presidential candidates came to be identified with major foreign policy change. They tended to bring in large numbers of their own people to implement those changes, and thus contributed to the in and out flow.

It's difficult to make historical comparisons because so many things are different. In 1960, Kennedy ran on the "missile gap" and a larger defense gap issue, just as Reagan ran on a defense gap issue in 1980. Kennedy shortly thereafter quietly abandoned the position when it became clear that in fact there was not a gap (even though many specialists believed that Kennedy was right at the time). It wasn't terribly hard for him to do so; he didn't have a large national following of people who were attached to that position and would denounce him for failure to do adhere to it.

In 1980, there was no question that, in certain weapons categories, the Soviets had superiority, but there was a lot of argument about the way Reagan formulated the issue. Reagan didn't seem to want to abandon his views about the defense gap, but if he had wanted to there would have been a large group of people—experts and non-experts—who followed these issues and would have cried betrayal. Thus, Reagan probably had less leeway.

*Question:* Did the media have a role to play in the emergence of a national security operation and the national security adviser's emergence in relationship to the State Department, or were these just reflecting other developments?

*Dr. Destler:* I think they've had a role in two large ways. First, reporting a fact makes it a bigger fact. Reporters said, correctly, that there was a conflict between Vance and Brzezinski in the Carter administration. But at the same time the fact that it was reported prominently tended to perpetuate and exacerbate the conflict. After all, where do most people in Washington who work in the government get their information about what is going on at the senior levels of government? They get it—whether it's information or misinformation—from reading *The Washington Post* or *The New York Times* in the mornings, the same place that we get it. So there is a reinforcing phenomenon here.

Second and more generally, the press played a role in the broader, societal opening-up process. In the first twenty years after World War II, the press that covered foreign policy and national security issues was anything but a muckraking press. There were some leaks and some impressive stories, but by and large the press believed that what the government said was true. The press was basically sympathetic and tended to be supportive of the main goals of foreign policy. Today the press has a greater propensity to challenge, a greater propensity to report things publicly. That has contributed to a more open and, I think, more polarized condition in the foreign policy community.

*Question:* Just a follow-up on that. Would you say that congressional determination to play a role in foreign policy also had something to do with changes in presidential staff levels?

*Dr. Destler:* Yes, in fact at the staff level some people who are coming to work for White House national security staffs now are people who have gotten their training in politics on Capitol Hill. They had joined the much expanded foreign policy staff of individual congressmen or congressional committees. There is a two-way flow. In 1980, for example, some people from the Carter administration went to Capitol Hill staff positions, with a considerable number coming the other way. There are considerably more staff jobs in Washington in which one can do foreign policy as a day-to-day business than there used to be.

That has interesting effects on the larger system. We ought to be better off because we've got more experts, we've got more analysis, we've got more resources. However, it also means we've got more people pushing their senators to introduce amendments in the legislative branch. We've got more people worrying that they don't want to get their boss, the secretary of state, into a room alone with the secretary of treasury, "because" to quote their staff aides' thoughts, "God knows what they will agree to and they won't know what they are talking about. We'll have to spend days straightening it out, so keep those guys apart." I'm exaggerating, but there is that real element. As you get more staff people, you do tend to have more of the actual business going through the staffs, and the principals sometimes find it harder. You also often find more competitiveness among the staffs and the principals; they find it harder to work things out. When you get a crucial national security issue, a real crisis, it always goes up to the level of the senior officials and most of the staff aides get squeezed out. There is a lot of business, however, that isn't conducted that way.

*Question:* To extend that line of thought in two ways: to what extent has the staff moved from an in-house and interagency operation to negotiating processes with contacts with Congress and with other governments? To what extent does this have an influence on what kind of advice is handed to the president?

*Dr. Destler:* That's a good question. Let me preface my answer by saying that I believe there is a need to draw upon what people in the public administration field have written about staff work, what is generally thought to be good government practice, what a staff aide like the national security assistant should do and what he or she shouldn't do.

I put together such a list in 1980. A whole set of things were in the "should" category: information gathering, analysis, monitoring, implementation, providing information. There was a "maybe" category which included things like background briefings for the press and discreet policy advocacy; the president can ask, "What do you really think?" and an aide can tell him.

But clear and very visible positions on policy issues were in the "should not" category, because the staff aide who makes those positions known is likely to skew the process of advice. A second "No" I listed was public prominence, a rule that Mc-Farlane is violating but without, so far I think, the cost to the system that I thought it would have had. The third thing in the "shouldn't do" category is what you mentioned, actual negotiations—not so much with Congress but with foreign governments. The national security advisor who was the most involved by far in policy negotiations which shut out other senior officials was, of course, Henry Kissinger. These negotiations had enormous costs for the operation of government; though they led to significant achievements.

Could we have had an opening to China with a different policy process? I think so, though others will disagree. If the White House staff role in negotiating becomes very visible or widespread it is particulaly pernicious because it means that everybody thinks they have to deal with the White House. It becomes very hard for anybody in the State Department to get any negotiating business done.

There has been a mixed situation, I think, under the current administration. McFarlane has been fairly active on Capitol Hill, which I'm not sure is entirely a bad thing. I think that previous presidential national security operations have suffered from not

having a good enough sense of congressional politics. I think
McFarlane seems to be an intelligent and capable reader of the
Hill. He did some good work during the Scowcroft Commission,
and in relating arms control positions to the MX missile. Whatever you think of the MX missile as an operating system, it was a
good connecting job. Apparently he was also one of the key
figures in the recent hostage resolution (the hijacking of a TWA jet
in Beruit). So far he hasn't taken over the main policy negotiations in the sense that Kissinger did, and he certainly hasn't acted
without the knowledge of the senior Cabinet people, again as
Kissinger did and Brzezinski was believed to be doing on occasions.

*Question:* Back in 1950 and 1951 when we were doing the
Brookings Institution study of the administration of foreign affairs
in overseas operations under contract with the Budget Bureau,
we tried to get information about the National Security Council
staff and what they were doing. In interviews they were very
unresponsive and completely unwilling to let us see any documentation. We didn't like to take their word for all the things they
said they were accomplishing as long as there was no backup.
And there wasn't much information in the press in those days.
After our book-length report came out, published by the Government Printing Office, Jimmy Lay and his staff got quite upset
because they thought we had mistreated them. Nowadays have
you found them more responsive, or are you relying largely on
the press? Do you ever see documentation?

*Dr. Destler:* I do not see lots of contemporary documentation.
Part of the problem is that the documentation is classified. In my
policy process research for publication, I do use not-for-attribu-
tion interviews fairly widely. However, my principle is that I
don't want to have to get what I'm going to write about declassi-
fied. What I have tried to do when I deal with a contemporary
administration is to rely on interviews with people involved, with
people who know something about what has happened, and
whatever other sources I can find, including the press. I double-
check this information where I can. For past administrations, I
look at presidential libraries, at least selectively, and I look at oral

histories: from the Truman, Eisenhower, Kennedy, and Johnson libraries.

As I told Ken earlier, I think the Miller Center's Carter administration oral history project is very interesting and important because the Center is pulling together a lot of information. Obviously, it won't be the central documentary collection (that will be the Carter Library), but gathering a mass of first-hand information about one presidency is useful. In general, I find that the patterns that one picks up from extensive interviewing are confirmed by the documentation that I've seen years later.

I have become a good friend of a man who, ten years after your Brookings report, had the responsibility of co-authoring with the same James Lay an official history of the National Security Council: Bob Johnson. I gather that it was not always entirely easy for him to co-author that document because of Lay's reluctance to put things on public record.

*Question:* It seems to me whenever anybody talks about the National Security Council, basically they're talking about foreign policy and the other half of national security, is certainly the military. The NSC and the national security staff have not had a director who was a military man or who had any significant military experience or study. And I also have the feeling that the NSC hasn't gotten into strategic planning much. They leave that pretty much to Defense. The director had all sorts of conflicts over the years with the secretary of state, but he never had any conflicts with the secretary of defense. What I'm trying to get at is: what is the role, if any, of the National Security Council staff in strategic policy? I mention this particularly in the light of my feeling, I may not be right about this, that we have been and are building up defense forces at an enormous rate, without any strategic plan. I don't know what kind of a war they anticipate fighting. It seems to me that this is something the NSC should get into. I'm sure that the secretary of the navy has a plan that nobody would agree with, including a six hundred ship navy. Why doesn't the NSC get into this sort of thing?

*Dr. Destler:* Your history is on the mark. There have been modest exceptions, but as a general rule the NSC has been much more involved in foreign policy than in defense policy. It is ironic because the institutional origins are, of course, in the National Security Act; and one of the original rationales for the National Security Council was that it might be an alternative to an intergrated Department of Defense. Truman used the NSC to deal with some issues involving the conduct of the Korean War, but he made his most serious war decisions in a more intimate advisory group.

The NSC staff played a role in 1983 on the MX missile, and Brzezinski played a role earlier in the Carter Doctrine deployment decision, but these weapons decisions were exceptional because they had become visible politically, related to arms control and other high-visibility foreign policy issues. We have had a general, Brent Scowcroft, at the head of the NSC staff. But your point is right. So the question becomes, why?

One reason is that presidents are much more involved in foreign policy. Another is the difficulty in getting a handle on the Defense Department. One of the better actual or at least potential handles on the military is the budget process, and to this the NSC has not given a lot of emphasis. Kissinger set up a strategic analysis staff, but it didn't have a lot of impact in his time. Even the Budget Bureau hasn't been able to develop much leverage on the Pentagon budget to date. At bottom, the problem may be the lack of incentives, of rewards for presidents and presidential aides who actually get into and grapple with those questions.

*Question:* Do you think they should?

*Dr. Destler:* Well, I would agree there is a problem, just as many people in Washington across a wide political spectrum, would agree with your earlier characterization: a lot is being spent and a lot is being built, and much more energy has been devoted to the build-up *per se* than to putting it within a coherent military strategy, a clear set of priorities. I think this needs to be done. I'm not sure the White House national security staff is the best place to do it. You might have a better prospect of achieving this it if you had a secretary of defense who was so minded, and then provided him with allies in a smaller unit in the White House, rather than trying to take this huge job away from the secretary entirely. I'm not sure it can be done from outside the Pentagon.

*Mr. Thompson:* Unless General Whitlach or somebody wants time for a rebuttal, we probably should declare the meeting adjourned. We are very grateful to Mac Destler for this full and clear presentation.

# The President and National Security*
PHILIP ODEEN

*Narrator:* Philip Odeen left the University of Wisconsin, completing graduate work there, and went to the Department of Defense where he worked in a variety of different positions. He became a principal deputy assistant secretary of defense and then went on to become director of program analysis in the National Security Council. Then he left the government but did not leave the area of national security policy. He has been involved consistently from the private sphere in important studies of military pension programs and of course this vital area of the relationship between the Department of State and the National Security Council in producing the Odeen Report. It is a pleasure to have you here at the Miller Center, Philip Odeen.

*Mr. Odeen:* I thought what I would do is talk in broad terms about the role of the National Security Council, going beyond the Carter administration experience which I had the opportunity to study for the President four years ago. There were a series of studies of the way the national security operation was organized within the Carter administration. I did one of the four studies which was on the relationship between the National Security Council and Defense, State, Arms Control and Disarmament Agency (ACDA), and other agencies. The other three studies were largely internal Department of Defense studies. In the process of this work I gave considerable thought to my own experiences on the Kissinger NSC staff and of course I have followed with some interest how the NSC has operated in the Reagan administration. So today I will talk in general terms about the role I see for the National Security Council in coordinating defense and national security policy, giving a number of examples. Then I'd be happy to respond to specific questions about the Carter experience or any other questions you may want to raise.

*Presented at the Miller Center on November 18, 1983.

In thinking about the role of the National Security Council and how it will operate in any administration, the first rule is that there are no set rules. Each president has his own personality, his own way of doing things, and his NSC is going to be different depending on his personality. But despite the flexibility you have to have to fit the structure to the personality of a president, there are some guidelines you simply have to address when trying to put together a National Security Council system. I see three primary considerations. First, there is no way to avoid bringing a number of tough questions to the president for a decision. When it comes time to make a decision on such issues as basing the MX or arms control policy, the president is going to have to get personally involved and he's going to have to make the decision. And so you have to have a system that when such issues arise, you can bring them to the president in a way he can make a rational decision.

Secondly, and not surprisingly, those types of decisions are not only complex, but they are often very political and very controversial. Therefore, the system must be structured to handle those kinds of questions. They will require analysis and thought—a lot of different aspects must be considered. In addition, you're going to have a variety of government agencies involved. It's not going to be a pure Department of Defense issue. In most cases, the State Department will be involved, the ACDA will be involved, and in these days, economic agencies such as Commerce and Treasury may be involved. So you have to have a process to bring to bear the perspectives and input of a number of departments.

And finally, once a decision is made, you need a means of following up to make sure that something really happens. In most cases this is a real shortcoming, the lack of follow-up to ensure the decision is implemented. In summary, you have to have an active NSC system. You have to have good people and you have to have enough structure and process to handle these complex and controversial problems.

Let me now be more specific about how you structure the NSC. The NSC staff plays two quite different roles. First, they have a role as personal staff to the president. The assistant to the president for national security affairs is the president's closest adviser on national security matters. No matter how close the president may be to the secretary of state or secretary of defense, over time the NSC adviser becomes the person he turns to in large part because of closeness. Their offices are literally only a few feet apart and they are usually together as issues develop. The National Security Council adviser will brief him daily, sometimes many times a day, and over time a close relationship develops. During the Nixon presidency, Secretary of State Rogers and Mr. Nixon were longtime and close personal friends. But within a very short period of time Henry Kissinger developed a very close relationship with the President and Rogers lost almost all of his influence with the President.

This personal role will vary from administration to administration. Each president is going to want to be served somewhat differently. Reagan by all accounts does not want to get into the issues deeply. He doesn't spend a lot of time on foreign policy and security issues. There have been exceptions; apparently he was very actively involved during the Grenada crisis. But up to that point he stayed away from the details of these issues.

Carter was the exact opposite. I've seen documents that went to President Carter for decision that were literally an inch thick, and Carter would read the entire document. From my point of view it made absolutely no sense, but he would slave away, getting to his office at 5:30 or 6:00 in the morning to go over all these documents and get into the details.

Nixon fell somewhere in between. He was a very organized person. We had to provide short memos, usually one page on a routine issue and a maximum of three pages, no matter how important it was. You could append added information, but with only three pages you had to be very focused on what the real issues were, what the key facts were and what the analysis said. You also had to outline the views of the various participants. It was a very structured and organized source of information that the President would supplement with discussions with Kissinger and others. Each president has his own way and you have to adapt the system to their way of doing business.

There is a second role for the NSC staff, which I call the institutional role. These responsibilities should not vary, regardless of the style of the president or how he wants to use the staff. This institutional role consists of a series of functions or tasks for the national security system, including the staff in the White

House, and participation by the other concerned agencies. I see four institutional tasks. The first is an obvious one: developing security policy. The NSC staff should oversee the development of clear policies that give direction to the agencies, a strategic framework for the agencies to develop their programs within. In addition, it is necessary to set priorities. I think you all recognize that resources are limited and often the agencies have to make choices. In making those choices, what are the president's priorities? Unless they are clear, the agency will use its own priorities.

This first role, setting policy, is usually a major part of the activity of the National Security Council in the opening months of a new administration. During the Nixon administration the vehicle was a National Security Study Memoranda. These NSSMs were orders from the President to do a particular piece of analysis or study of a particular problem. About seventy-five of these memos were issued in the first year of the Nixon administration. An enormous amount of activity was devoted to analysis of our policy alternatives and to coming up with policy recommendations on particular issues. This effort resulted in a broad framework of specific policies, ranging from broad national security priorities down to policies for a region such as NATO or the Middle East, and in some cases to policies for certain key countries. Some of this massive effort was in fact make-work. Kissinger, to an extent, used this as a way to keep the bureaucracy busy doing studies and therefore less apt to challenge the things he was trying to do. But it was also a serious effort and it resulted in a sound set of policies which were laid out to guide administration programs.

The Carter administration followed a somewhat similar approach. They changed the name, calling them Policy Research Memoranda (PRM). About thirty of these studies were done at first, some broad ones while others were narrow. Some of these studies were quite good but others were far less carefully done than the Nixon administration studies. One important study, called PRM 10, was designed to lay out a basic national security framework. It was, unfortunately, quite unsuccessful. The Nixon staff, for a variety of reasons I could talk about later, had done a better job. But some of the Carter studies were well done and at least they made a serious effort to set out a series of policies for the administration to follow.

It is surprising that the Reagan administration did not go through this phase and did not do a series of broad policy studies. While they did a few focused studies, at the end of their first year they didn't have a policy framework per se. In part this was because there was broad agreement on approach among many of the key officials. The President and probably Richard Allen and Cap Weinberger and others generally agreed on what they wanted to do, but they didn't codify these policies or lay them out clearly for the bureaucracy, and they did not set any real priorities. I don't think they fully recognized at that point the reality of fiscal constraints. The feeling was the economy was going to rebound quickly and strongly and national security was so important that we could spend whatever was necessary on defense and priorities were really not necessary. They didn't think a lot about the need to make choices at that point in time. Also they were emphasizing the role of the Cabinet, giving much more responsibility to the departments, with less power centralized in the White House. They carried this out to a large degree, and therefore they were less interested in centrally directed studies or the development of a central policy framework.

Another factor was that the key staff people in the Reagan administration had quite different backgrounds than those in the Carter and Nixon administrations. For the most part they were non-professionals in the sense of not having broad government experience. They came from a variety of backgrounds and many of them had very strong views on issues. I don't want to use the word "ideologue" in a pejorative sense—but they had strong ideological views on many national security issues. A number were specialists with particularly strong views on a specific issue: nuclear proliferation, Taiwan, China, the Soviet Union, and so on. They had a number of individuals with a "mission" to achieve something in a particular area. They did not have many people who thought broadly or in strategic terms. They also had few people who understood how the bureaucracy operated. Therefore, I don't think they thought in terms of a policy framework that would set some bounds for the departments and control the way decisions were made.

During the second year, after Judge Clark moved to the NSC, a study of broad national security strategy was finally done. I've not seen it because it was classified but Judge Clark gave a fairly full exposition of the strategy at a speech at the Georgetown Center in the spring of 1982. It was, in my view and the view of many others, a variety of basically broad goals and platitudes. It did not set priorities or make clear what choices were to be made if everything couldn't be done. It was a very general framework and I doubt that it helped very much when it came time to make tough decisions on weapons systems or allocations of dollars or other resources. But regardless, that's the first role—developing policy—and I think a very important one.

The second role the NSC plays, an important but sometimes a a neglected one, is forcing decisions on key issues. It's very easy with a job in the White House on the National Security Council staff to be swept along by the flood of papers that come from the departments to the White House for attention. There is an endless flow of things that the president has to decide, new policy, proposals, and other actions that couldn't be handled in six or seven days a week, twelve hours a day. But in my view, at least, you have a responsibility to do more, that is, to try to reach down and find issues that will really have some impact on the future of the country. Such questions should be pulled up out of the bureaucracy, analyzed and decisions made if decisions in fact are called for.

There is a saying that I heard from General Andy Goodpaster who was a key military aide to President Eisenhower. Eisenhower used to say, and I think is very apt in this case, something to the effect that "critical" issues, that is things that are very time urgent, are seldom truly important. On the other hand, the really important issues are seldom time urgent. There is a constant flow of items which people insist you must decide on today, cables that must go immediately to an embassy or a letter that has to be sent in response to this or that. They all seem very time urgent and very critical at the time. But in fact they don't really have much impact on the future of the country. Yet there are fundamental issues, just sitting out there, that ought to be looked at but everyone is too busy to examine them. Many of you are business people and I know that you understand that these kinds of issues arise in the business world as well.

So the second role of the NSC staff is to reach down and focus on those problems and surface them up for analysis. An example of such an issue that should have been addressed by the Reagan administration was the long-term affordability of the defense program they embarked on.

They began with very large, real increases in spending and they pushed two budgets through the Congress with those kinds of increases. They're fighting today for their third increase, the defense budget for 1984. The Congress had made substantial cuts in that budget and made it clear they will do the same next year. There is a fight going on within the Pentagon right now over the 1985 budget. There are very wide differences between the dollars the Defense Department wants and what the OMB people say makes sense and is affordable. If the dollars continue to be cut back substantially many of the programs they've begun are going to be difficult to support. Moreover, if you do support them, other things that are very important will have to suffer. I don't think the Reagan people thought through the affordability of their defense effort. It's not a really complicated problem, but was something they had to address early on, but didn't.

Another such issue that deserves to be surfaced is the role of the Navy. The Navy had always been the most difficult element of the Defense Department to plan rationally. They have a wide variety of missions, an officer corps with strong views, and a lot of political clout. Few White House staffs or even secretaries of defense have been very successful in getting control of the direction of the Navy, what purposes and missions we want the Navy for, what kind of forces we should have, what priorities ought to be set. Again, this is an issue deserving of attention by the National Security Council, but is not the kind of issue that often gets raised. But it's an example of the second role: forcing decisions on key issues.

The third role is obvious, that is managing the decision process. The issues the NSC copes with are difficult, complicated, and often very controversial. You need a process to make sure that all of the participants who ought to have a say, have a say. The State Department will have views on defense issues and vice versa; the Arms Control and Disarmament Agency will also often have ideas to contribute and more often these days the issues have substantial economic consequences. Therefore you've got to get the Commerce or Treasury staffs into the decision process. You need a process that elicits these views in some rational fashion and provides good analysis where analysis is called for. Also the NSC staff must quality control the analysis to make sure it's being done well, that the right options are developed, and that the material is stated fairly. Finally you have to put the material together so that the Cabinet officers and the president can understand it and make decisions.

One of the shortcomings I found in the Carter administration's NSC system was a very chaotic process in terms of managing the analysis and the decision process. Meetings were held constantly involving the secretaries of defense and state, the head of the CIA and other senior people. They did not do good preparatory work. Papers to educate the key officials weren't completed early so they could review them adequately before meeting. After I completed the draft of the report on the Carter NSC system, I met with the senior people in the departments to discuss the report and get their reactions and comments. We were talking about this particular problem and Cy Vance was lamenting the fact that, as he said, "It seems like I go to a meeting every day." I went back and checked and it turned out during the first year of the Carter administration they had one of these high-level meetings involving the key players each week. The second year they had two. The third year (1979) when I was doing my study, they had four per week, a terrible burden. Secretary Vance said, "My preparation usually is in the car going from the State Department to the White House. I'm sure most of you've been both places and know they are not very far apart." He said his aide sat next to him and gave him a one page paper to read. "With that I walk into the meeting and try to discuss this issue intelligently." This was partly a function of too many meetings and partly a function of not having papers done in advance, a process problem. Busy people can't always sit down two hours before a meeeting and do their homework. They have to have the material the weekend before when they have some spare time or at least the night before so they can read it.

The papers during this period were not on time and not well done. The result was a lot of wasted motion. Frank Carlucci, who was the deputy director of the CIA, had this way of describing how it was. He said, "We go unprepared to a meeting, the issues aren't well formulated, the key problems haven't been identified and we spend an hour and a half in a meeting. By the time the meeting is over we have figured out what the real issues are and we say, O.K., we'll come back tomorrow and meet again to address them." This was a serious process problem, the kind of thing a good NSC system simply shouldn't let happen.

The final step in the process is to pull all this information together for the president. It must be done in some fashion so he can make sense out of it and make a rational decision. This is an important responsibility, it's time consuming and it's demanding. The key here is that you have an evenhanded, fair approach. You can't favor the State Department or the Pentagon or somebody else. You've got to give everybody a fair shake. If the key players don't feel they had a chance to have their say or that their views were't accurately presented to the president, they have the incentive to go outside the system. They will leak things to the press or run up to the Hill. If you can give the agencies an opportunity to participate they are much more apt to play the game and go along with the decision when it's made.

The final role for the NSC staff is ensuring decisions are implemented. This is perhaps the most neglected area of all. In government there is a great drive to be involved in making big policy or program decisions. Everybody wants to play. Enormous amounts to time and effort are spent on these decisions, analyzing them, arguing, revising drafts, and so forth. But once a decision is made people assume it's going to take care of itself. The implementation is relegated to much lower levels of the organization after the decision is made.

One of the things I noted after I left the government and went into the business world was that the process in the business world is almost reversed. This is not to say that business people don't focus on policy decisions or don't think about strategy issues. But once a decision is made they then make sure that whatever the decision is, that it is carried out effectively and efficiently. A reasonable decision well carried out has a lot more pay-off in the long run than a brilliant decision sloppily implemented. This is a point that the governmnet has never quite figured out. And it's a problem throughout the government, and not just in the White House.

There is an important role for the NSC staff in follow-up and monitoring. I don't mean to say that they ought to implement but they ought to follow up to make sure that decisions are in fact carried out. This would involve follow-up memos asking for reports, spending time with the agencies checking on implementation plans. You need a process to check on implementation. To do this is tough, it takes time, and it always gets the last priority. It's hard to know what really happens in organizations as big as the Defense and State Departments. It's important to have people on the NSC staff who have spent a good bit of their lives in those organizations and have the knowledge of how they work; they know the key people, they know how to get information, who to get answers from. If you have those kinds of people on the staff, if they're told that implementation or follow-up is important and that it has priority, your program and policy decisions are going to have a much greater impact.

There are a couple of examples of poor follow-up during the Carter administration that I came across when I was doing the study. One of the early studies done by the Carter administration was on the military threat and force needs in the Persian Gulf. They did a careful analysis of what the needs might be in the Gulf, which they saw as a high risk and high priority area. The Iranian situation was serious, although the Shah was still in charge. The analysis said that over the long term substantial threats in that area were likely, and U.S. military forces were likely to be required. The President directed Defense to pull together a small, highly mobile force, and prepare plans to deploy to that area if needed. A year and a half or so went by and when the Iranian crisis really erupted they found that little had happened. The force had not been created although some low-level actions had gone on. If we had needed to put forces in at that time it would have been a very, very difficult situation. In discussing the implementation issue with Harold Brown, he commented to me that in retrospect, "If somebody on the NSC staff had been bugging us, if Brzezinski had called me occasionally to ask, 'What are you doing on that?' or if a senior NSC staff person had talked to my senior people and asked for reports, we probably would have been in much better shape than we were at that time if there had been some follow-up. It turned out not to matter because we didn't have to use force in the Gulf. But if we would have had to, it could have been a difficult situation."

Another more personal example was the fairly long report, I guess sixty or seventy pages, that I drafted on my NSC study. It was sent to Carter two different times and in his way of doing things, he read the report from beginning to end both times. The first time he asked Brzezinski to request comments from the secretary of defense, state and other key players. I knew he read it because I saw the copy with his question marks and comments in the margin. After it was sent out for comment, they sent the President another memo which said, "These are the various issues and the views of the agencies on each, they agree on this and they disagree on that." Carter reread the report because I again saw a copy of it and he had marginal notes all the way through it. It would say, "I agree, do this, this should happen," etc. He accepted most of my recommendations and gave very clear directions for action on the margins of the report. As far as I know little ever happened.

This was a year or more before the end of the administration. Brzezinski did not agree with most of my recommendations probably because many of them were critical of his management. I cited what I thought were shortcomings in the way things were working and he was not very happy about it. He simply ignored it, and as best I could tell, there was no follow-up process, nobody worrying about such things. Carter had no way of knowing whether anything happened and I suspect that was typical for most decisions of this type.

Washington humor can be pretty tough and there were a lot of Carter jokes. There are Polish jokes, Aggie jokes and North Dakota jokes. There were also Carter jokes floating around Washington at that time. My favorite is the one about Carter, Giscard and Schmidt at a summit meeting. A group of terrorists invaded the summit and captured all three world leaders and decided as an example to execute them by firing squad. First they lined up Giscard against the wall. The terrorist soldiers readied their rifles, the sergeant in charge said, "Ready, aim,"—Giscard, being a pretty shrewd guy, yelled, "Earthquake!" Everybody dove for cover and Giscard escaped over the fence. They next lined Schmidt up and went through the same process. The sergeant said, "Ready, aim," and Schmidt yells, "Tornado!" Again everyone heads for cover and Schmidt escaped over the fence.

They then put Carter up against the wall and went through the same process. "Ready, aim," and Carter yells, "Fire!" That was probably a very unfair joke but it had elements of truth.

*Narrator:* We ought to let you know that some of this problem of follow-up and time is also an issue in the educational world, as I'm sure you know. A colleague who has been unstinting in his willingness to take on duties in the University and in the department, and who happens to be in this room, once remarked that the first year he was here, having considerable duties in addition to his teaching, he didn't have time to do his own research. The second year he was here he didn't have time to read the newspaper in the morning before he went into class. The third year he was here he didn't have time even to look at his notes before he began his lectures, so there are issues of this kind that come up in every setting. Who'd like to ask the first question?

*Question:* The international conferences that President Ford and President Carter are having, the one in Vail and the last one in Atlanta, do you think they will serve a useful purpose, and how do you think their views will be utilized?

*Mr. Odeen:* My guess is probably not. There is no way that those meetings have much impact. I know a little bit about the one in Vail and who was there. They are stimulating, fun, interesting kinds of experiences. The problem is after they are held there is no follow-up. Usually there are very few government officials there in attendance—just former officials. As a result there is nobody involved that can make something happen. They may issue a report which they will send out but the chances are it won't be read. The meetings have some educational value and I take part in these things from time to time. They are a lot of fun but I don't really think they accomplish an awful lot except for some education. You often have people there who will be involved in a future administration, and are there because the background is useful. Business people also attend and their education on issues is useful because they have ways to influence future actions. But other than this general kind of background education for people who later may have some opportunity to use the experience, it's just very hard to see how they are very useful.

*Question:* I worked for lend-lease in World War II in Cairo and Egypt and I had peripheral familiarity with the British secretariat system. It was extremely effective in coordinating the military, the diplomatic, and so forth. Are you familiar with that and the history and development of it because it seems they are far more effective at doing that than we are.

*Mr. Odeen:* I don't know much about the history of it but I know a bit how it has operated over the last ten years or so. I agree. They are much better and more tightly organized. They also have far fewer political appointees involved in the process. In a department you'd have a cabinet officer who is a member of Parliament and maybe one or two others. Occasionally someone is brought in from the outside to advise the minister. But you rely on a cadre of civil servants and you've got a permanent secretary who is very experienced.

*Question:* You have a continuity.

*Mr. Odeen:* You have much more continuity, that's right.

*Question:* And they know all the relevant people in the various agencies. Isn't that right?

*Mr. Odeen:* It's a very elitist kind of organization which has its drawbacks and problems. But the people who get to the senior civil servants roles have spent their life there. They are virtually all out of the same educational system—Oxford, Cambridge, the same kind of background—public schools and all that. This may be changing to some extent, but they have worked together for a very long time. They also have a person who works directly for the prime minister who is the most senior of the civil servants, who is the cabinet secretary. Again this is a very distinguished career civil servant who pulls things together for the prime minister. So you've got this "old boys" or "old girls" network, really an "old boys" network in this case, I suspect, that makes things happen.

*Question:* The same system exists in business with the development since the 1920s of the management committee, which is widespread in all businesses now. It develops a policy and implements it because the people are the same.

*Mr. Odeen:* And most of them also have continuity. In most large companies there is a lot of continuity in top management. I'm thinking particularly of IBM or General Electric or AT&T or General Motors—they are career people with their firm. It is less true in some of the consumer products businesses. People move in and out and marketing people move in and out. But even there they often have years of experience with the company. The average Cabinet officer or subcabinet officer in the U.S. government has a tenure of about two years. There is an awful lot of turnover and it's very hard to have continuity with that kind of turnover.

The other consideration with the British system is that the members of the cabinet are members of Parliament and they have been in the Parliament for a long time. They may have had responsibility in the shadow cabinet for that area when they were out of office. There is just a lot more continuity in this system than we have. I am sure there are disadvantages, too, in terms of fewer fresh ideas, new approaches and so on. But in terms of coordinating things and making things happen there is a big advantage.

*Question:* It is somewhat alarming to casual observers sitting in this peaceful place and realizing that the National Security Council is operating on what appears to be such an ad hoc basis. Could you comment on what you perceive to be the difference in broad terms between the approach to this fundamental question of security in this country and the way it is approached in Russia?

*Mr. Odeen:* I'm certainly no expert on Russia but my impression is that you have people who have been in that business for very, very long periods of time. The average age of the senior leadership in the Soviet Union is much higher than it is here. If you look at the senior people in the politburo and the central committee, you find people who have been in those roles for very long periods of time. Their generals and admirals tend to be much older, much more senior than our people. In the American military generals tend to retire at age fifty-five. Even a four-star general gets out at fifty-seven or fifty-eight and the Soviet generals are often in their seventies. On the civilian side you have the same kind of continuity. In that case, I think it may be a problem. There is too much continuity and they have great difficulty in taking new directions and doing things differently. But you have a very stable kind of situation as opposed to the much greater turbulence we have.

Soviet military matters are largely decided within the military bureaucracy. There is far less of a role for the civilian. Big issues, big decisions come to the politburo for decision but the details that the Soviet civilians know about with respect to what goes on in the military is very, very limited. During the first strategic arms limitation talks that started in 1969, most of the participants on the Soviet side were diplomats. The discussions got into considerable detail on such questions as the numbers of missiles, their characteristics and capabilities and other highly technical issues. I remember Paul Nitze, who was one of the participants at that time as he is today, telling me how nervous the Soviet military delegates were about these issues even being raised in these secret negotiations. They felt these were not issues that diplomats ought to know anything about or had any right to know about. Their military would talk to our military and say, "We shouldn't be covering these issues. These are not the kind of things that diplomats ought to talk about." Finally Paul Nitze put out a briefing for the Soviet diplomats on their forces—how many missiles they had, what type, how big they were, and where they were located, the whole picture. Nitze briefed the Soviet delegation on their strategic forces. That had to be a unique development. But the Soviet civilian side just had very little involvement or knowledge in such matters.

Obviously there is involvement at the top, at the very senior Soviet levels, on big issues such as resource allocations, any major new deployments or involvement overseas, perhaps some involvement in large weapons systems issues, but very little. The Soviet defense ministry really makes most decisions. They are given a piece of the pie, apparently a modest amount of real ruble growth each year. They can take those funds and do with it what they want within some very broad policy. This situation is very different in our case. There is a much broader civilian involvement, both within the Pentagon and at the government-wide level. At the senior civilian levels you have a lot less continuity because every four years you have a whole new team coming in.

Within the Pentagon, the top civilians may turn over but there is still a fair amount of continuity at senior levels. Many of the senior defense officials stay in the government for three or four years, they get out for three or four years and come back in again. So there is more continuity in fact than it sometimes might appear. One of the stabilizing factors is that below the Cabinet level, you have a lot of expertise and experience even among political appointees because they do tend to come and go. This is particularly true in Defense. At State you've got diplomatic people in a lot of the senior positions. So in the national security area at least you have a fair amount of continuity. It's not quite as ad hoc as it might seem to a casual observer.

*Question:* There is an old sequel of the story about the negotiations. After the meeting the Soviet delegate took Nitze aside and chided him for doing it because he said the Russian civilians didn't really need to know that.

Students of the presidency have frequently commented that the problem of presidential leadership is becoming enormously difficult because the pressure of daily events make it difficult for the president to devote his attention only to major issues. My question is whether or not in the way it operates that the office of the national security adviser and the increasingly substantial staff don't make that problem more difficult rather than less difficult in terms of foreign policy problems. That is to say, don't they make it more difficult for the president to push part of the decision process on lesser issues out of the White House and tend to accede to the enormous pressure of the media who want to know exactly what the president thinks about every little dinky issue? I just wonder if there has ever been a national security adviser who took the position that this issue is not important enough, let's get that back out of the White House, instead of, as they usually do, seeing themselves as competitors with the secretary of state and not wanting to seem to be less involved or less informed about a breaking issue. Institutionally, don't they make it more difficult rather than less difficult for the president to devote his attention only to high priority issues?

*Mr. Odeen:* Yes, I think there is something about the American psyche. Mrs. Odeen and I were at a dinner last night for Admiral Snavely. He is a British admiral whose title is Commander of the Combined Fleets, which I think is a wonderful name. He is the number two British Navy admiral. We were talking before dinner and he was making that point exactly. One of the things he said was, "What amazes me about American military leaders is they can never admit they don't know the answer. They have to be briefed on every trivial issue because if somebody comes and asks them a question they have got to be able to say that the answer is a, b, and c." He said, "It doesn't bother me a bit. There is no problem in my organization nor am I looked down on if somebody asks me a question, and I say I don't know, I'll find out for you. I will get an answer and get back to you. But there is something about American military people and I think, civilians as well; you've got to be on top of all the issues. You've got to look like you are knowledgeable, you are current, you've got a view and so on."

*Question:* Members of Congress these days, too. It didn't used to be the case in the House but now it seems they feel they have to know everything about everything.

*Mr. Odeen:* There is something about our psychology. I don't know what the reason could be. But I think that's right. We aren't willing to say some issues are not important, leave that to the Pentagon or State Department or the Navy or Army or somebody else.

*Question:* I think my question grows out of this last discussion. I suppose we are all troubled by the apparently universal problem of our being so preoccupied with the little things that we never have time for the big things. After World War II, I think, the State Department set up a policy planning staff with the intent and hope that that small group of people could be insulated from the affairs of the day and put their minds to the big issues for the future. I don't know if anyone thinks that worked well. My impression is that most people are not insulated; it breaks down, and they get involved in current operations. Do you have any wisdom on how this problem can be solved or whether the NSC has in fact achieved anything in helping to divorce the president from the smaller issues and enabling him to face the big ones ahead of time?

*Mr. Odeen:* The policy planning staff is a good example of how difficult it is to do that. Most people find when they get in such a position that it's a wonderful idea but you then find that the long-term issues you are worrying about are not what the secretary of state is worrying about. You can't stand not to have an input on all of the important things he is focused on or vice versa. The secretary says, "Hey, there are a bunch of smart people there. Why don't you get me some help from them on this problem that's pressing right now?" The next thing you know the planners are really into the loop on most issues.

I don't think there is any easy answer to this problem. To some extent, I thought Kissinger—when I worked for him at least—forced us to try to think through for him periodically what the big issues were, to lay out what we thought we ought to do about them in terms of whether there ought to be a study or some kind of analysis done, if we knew enough about it, whether it was something that ought to be addressed. Periodically, he went through a drill within the staff to try to step back a little bit and look at these issues. I am not sure how effective it was. In the Kissinger era, and to an extent during the Carter administration, they spent time during that period after the election and before the inauguration to lay out the really big issues that should be addressed and how they were going to look at them and make policy choices. That menu was the first group of national security study memoranda that were issued. But once you get into office I don't know how you maintain that broader view. It's so easy to get swept up in the details and fire drills.

One approach to the implementation question that I should have mentioned earlier, that somebody ought to look at is an Eisenhower administration group called the Operations Coordinating Board. The OCB had the responsibility for follow-up and ensuring that policies were carried out. It was chaired by the under secretary of state who was the number two person at State at that time. Although there were some mixed views on how well it worked, at least you had an institutionalized, senior-level group that was worrying about follow-up and implementation. I think that's something worth taking a look at again to see if that may be a way to get more attention to the question of implementation.

*Question:* Will you sharpen our understanding of the political and organizational role of NSC a little bit by saying more about two of the functions that you stated that NSC has: one, forcing decisions on key issues and the other one the implementing of decisions? Why aren't those two functions in particular functions that belong to the relevant department? Why isn't it the State or Defense Department's function to force decisions on key issues or to implement decisions once they're made?

*Mr. Odeen:* In some cases they do force decisions, if it's an issue they feel needs to be addressed. In other cases there may be great reluctance on their part to get the White House involved in those issues. They may not want to surface them, preferring to take care of the problems themselves. For example, the Navy doesn't want any help in deciding what ships they ought to buy or how they ought to be structured. They don't even want the secretary of defense's help, let alone the NSC staff or the president. There is resistance to getting the office of the secretary of defense involved in Navy matters, let alone let the State Department or the White House or having somebody else muck around with those issues. With many of the tough issues, there are all kinds of bureaucratic considerations; once you raise them up to a higher level you lose control, and you don't want to lose control over those things if they're important to you. If you don't absolutely have to go to the president for a decision or if you can find a way to address a question in a generalized kind of way that keeps them out of the nitty-gritty of what you're doing, you have a bureaucratic incentive to do that.

*Question:* But in that case that sounds like a management problem within Defense.

*Mr. Odeen:* Well, it is but the reluctance may be on the part of the secretary of defense, too. The secretary of defense isn't always anxious to get the White House involved and the secretary of state is even less anxious in some cases to get the White House involved in deciding what our policy ought to be toward the Iran situation, for example. Consider the Brzezinski/Vance battles over our policy vis-à-vis Iran. State would have been very happy to have moved ahead without such issues ever being raised in the White House for a decision. The feeling is, it's our issue, we know what ought to be done, we don't want White House involvement. For God's sake, the NSC or Defense will get involved or Treasury or CIA or somebody else and we don't want that. Let's take care of that problem ourselves. We don't want to wash our dirty linen in front of the rest of the administration.

As far as implementation is concerned, it has to be done by the secretary of defense, or state or some other agency head. You can't, however, leave it entirely to them. In some cases the policy decision will be actively or passively opposed by a lot of people in the agencies. Unless you follow up periodically there are numerous opportunities to sabotage the decision or simply to drag one's feet and make sure that nothing happens. I don't mean to say that you can implement from the White House—you can't because you've got a very small staff—but some kind of follow-up on important issues is important.

It's also a problem within the agencies. Shy Meyer, who just retired as Chief of Staff of the Army, at a meeting recently was talking about this problem. As Chief of Staff of the Army, he spent virtually all his time on program and budgetary issues and the Congress. He said: "That's all I did. I only worried about developing the budget, addressing budget issues, and then addressing them the second and third time, and finally testifying on the Hill and going back again. I had no time for implementation. We paid almost no attention to what happened in terms of implementation. I knew that was wrong; I knew I should be spending time following up, making sure things were happening." He went on, "That's why all the scandals arise, the $1,100 plastic cans. The people at the top are too busy to worry about implementation. They're diverted by all these other things." As he put it, "The little old ladies in tennis shoes go and implement all these things and the people at senior levels don't have time to worry about what they do."

*Question:* It is also a consequence of another very important problem of continuity lately, and that is we don't have continuity at the top. We've had so much turnover. Being president is one of the most temporary jobs in town and so maybe it's natural for the agency to try and protect itself, try to rely on its own continuity because you know when the top fellow changes you're going to get more changes in the leadership among the political executives heading the agency so you try to protect yourself within the agency and prevent those big decisions from going up there because God knows what's going to happen.

*Mr. Odeen:* I think that's exactly right. The Navy case that I mentioned earlier is a great example. The Navy is a very conservative organization; they're not open to change, they are very confident; they know what they want to do. The Ford administration is going to want to do this and then Carter has a different idea and Reagan is going to want to do something else. We're going to get pulled here and there. This is a real problem with programs for building ships. They take eight years to build and are useful for thirty years. You can't afford to have all these wild policy and program swings and I'm sure that's a legitimate reason why they want to keep the political leaders out of the issues. I'm sure the same is true in the State Department. The professionals have a view of what our policy ought to be toward South America or Africa or Southeast Asia. They let the people in the White House worry about NATO, China, and the other sexier issues. But let us maintain control over policy in these less central areas.

*Question:* I apologize for this question. However, during the Grenada invasion which President Reagan led, our policy seems to disagree with the British and the British didn't like it. One of the statements made by a member of the staff on this very problem was that what you say in public usually differs from what you agree to privately. Based on this and since this Forum is more private than public, I want to find out from you whether you really perceive an interest in a change of government in any

African country. We have a so-called Marxist leadership in
Angola, Mozambique, and Ethiopia. Do they really pose any
threat? If so, how do you see it privately?

*Mr. Odeen:* I know so little about Africa that I really hesitate
to even try to answer your question. Most of my experience has
been with Western European issues and Asian issues, mostly
Southeast Asia and China to some degree. I know nothing about
the African situation. Certainly those countries don't pose any
very direct threat to us. There is no way we could say that. But
that area has a lot of resources that are important to us. You can
say there is an indirect threat in terms of availability of resources
or impact of shortages on price levels. But I just don't know
enough about that and I hesitate to answer. I'm sorry.

*Question:* You mean it's really not a military threat.

*Mr. Odeen:* No, no way.

*Question:* Mr. Odeen, there have been a number of things that
have really troubled me about the National Security Council
since it was formed in July of 1947. First of all, I think it has gone
way beyond the role that Congress designated for it and the
specific groundwork for having it, and the reasons for having it.
We've seen Dr. Kissinger preempt the role of Secretary of State
Rogers and the same thing with Brzezinski and Cyrus Vance.
Now is there any inherent danger here, a terrible danger, of who
speaks for the nation—the president, the secretary of state, or the
chairman of the security council? Can we not trim it back
severely and put some of that work back in the Cabinet officer's
role or the agencies? Or is this thing going to go like a rogue
elephant?

*Mr. Odeen:* No question about it. The role is much broader
and more pervasive than anybody thought in 1947. Some of that is
inevitable. There are a lot of reasons for it. First of all, foreign
policy has become a major political issue. It's no longer a
bipartisan matter or above politics. In fact, it has become a great
opportunity for presidents to build their prestige and standing.
The fact that Reagan will probably go to China in April next year

has an awful lot more to do with the upcoming election (1984) than it does with foreign policy or our relations with the Chinese. The political importance and significance that foreign policy now has has forced the president to be involved. He is much more concerned about managing foreign policy, to have some control over it. If you let the agencies handle it, you must be concerned about getting burned.

There are some substantive reasons, too. The complexity of most of the policy issues today is much greater than it was twenty-five or thirty years ago. In particular the economic implications of foreign policy and security issues have increased greatly. Some people argue that there really are no pure foreign policy issues, and I suspect that's right. But there are almost no issues that don't have at least some economic implications. Our security policy in the Far East is heavily tied to our relationship with Japan and our economic policies. The problems with trade with the Soviet Union, technology transfer, and a variety of other issues that have increased in importance, have major economic as well as security and foreign policy aspects. Yesterday in the final action on the Defense budget, Congress cut out one particular weapons system which it turns out is one of the very few major items we are buying from the Europeans. If you must cut something, you always cut something made overseas not in the United States. That's going to create a foreign policy problem. It's going to be very embarrassing for the White House and the administration and for the State Department. Most issues have gotten so intertwined, you can't say, "State Department, you handle it" anymore. You need to have the other agencies involved and once you get several agencies involved somebody has to manage that process and pull it together and help the president make a decision.

And finally, the time frame in the defense area has gotten so much longer and the dollar implications are so much greater. Making a decision to buy a ship used to be easy. It took two or three years to build and it wasn't very expensive. Now the technology is so complex and costs so great that you are making long-term commitments that tends to lead people to centralize things. As the decisions get bigger there is greater tendency toward centralization. The problem is that given there are substantive reasons for making many centralized top-level decisions in the White House environment, how do you keep driving down the less important issues to the agencies so you don't choke yourself with a flood of minor problems. It's hard to do.

*Question:* History records that Truman and Johnson knew very little about what was going on in the inner sanctum when we had a tragedy, the loss of our president. The press seems to think that we're going to have a rather senior citizen as president. My question is how much is the vice president involved in the security council at the present time compared to the Carter administration, because it seems to me that if the vice president is not involved and we have a tragedy, a double tragedy.

*Mr. Odeen:* Sure, but I think it varies a lot between administrations. When I was working on the NSC staff in the early seventies, the view was, thank God Spiro Agnew was not involved. The only time I ever saw him was on the elevator in the Old Executive Office Building. He did show up at the National Security Council meetings but they were *pro forma* events that didn't really matter that much. We seldom sent him copies of papers and he wasn't involved in any of the important, smaller meetings as far as I know. He had almost no role in the security area.

*Question:* It turns out he was busy but not at being vice president.

*Mr. Odeen:* I believe that it has been quite different with Mondale and Bush. They've been quite actively involved. Bush obviously has an interest, having been in China and at the UN as an ambassador and heading the CIA. He has a lot of background. He has an experienced and able foreign service officer as his national security adviser. He goes to meetings and chairs one of the important committees; he's in charge of the crisis management committee in the White House and was apparently actively involved in both the Lebanon and the Grenada crises. Bush has been quite centrally involved and I suspect will continue to be so. Mondale was somewhat less involved, perhaps because he didn't have the background. But he was quite actively involved compared to many vice presidents. He did attend meetings; he read papers and had a good staff of experienced people to support him. So the last two vice presidents at least have been quite intimately involved.

*Question:* I think I'll have to ask you to help me formulate my question as one that you may not wish to answer. It has to do in the broadest terms with the jurisdiction, either operational or philosophical, of the National Security Council. Does the council address the relationship of the potential impact on the security of this country and others to religious or philosophical problems that arise in the world? Specifically, as I understand it, there is about twenty-five percent of the world population that is Islamic oriented in one way or another in different sects. Our approach to security has been focused primarily on armament, who's got the biggest guns and who's got the most bombs. But this was not fundamental in the trigger point of the Iran problem. This was not the problem that was so devastating on the Marine contingent, but it was more a philosophical one, and it has to do with those areas of political entities where religious philosophies are concurrent with the governmental administration. This is generally so in communist countries and it is certainly so in Islamic ones. Is this a question that would be deliberated by the security council and if not, who in our government is considering it?

*Mr. Odeen:* I think that's a good issue. One of the problems, of course, is that we essentially have amateur officials who come into the government for a few years and go out again. They don't have that kind of background. You can be a very good administrator or an effective businessman, but you're not liable to be very knowledgeable on those kinds of issues. And yet they are clearly important. Understanding Communist ideology and how it affects senior officials in the Soviet Union or in China is very important in making sound decisions. What we have to rely on is the State Department and the CIA. In addition to State's people, the CIA has an extensive cadre of analysts who have spent their entire careers studying particular areas. They usually have good academic backgrounds and interact with the academic community. There is a group of China scholars who have had quite an impact on our thinking on China over the last fifteen years as we've gone through quite a basic policy change.

You have to rely on those kind of people. The trick is how do you make sure their views are surfaced and considered? One way you do that is through the staffing of the NSC. I mentioned earlier the need to have people that come out of the agencies. I don't think you want more than fifty professionals on the NSC staff, which is roughly the size it has been the last fifteen years. You don't want all fifty to be from State or Defense or CIA. But you want a cadre of people who came out of those agencies, who are able, experienced, knowledgeable, respected within their agencies. They often are the conduit for such information. They are the ones who take a little think piece that some smart analyst in the CIA writes on religious problems in Iran and gives it to Brzezinski to read at night or Cy Vance to read over a weekend. They make sure that such issues are brought out in the policy papers and not submerged. It's very informal. I don't know how you institutionalize it. You just have to count on having some of those bright, knowledgeable people on that NSC staff.

When I was involved on the NSC in the early seventies we had an absolutely first-rate staff. The caliber was much better than the Carter administration and head and shoulders better than the Reagan administration NSC staff. The quality of the NSC staff at present is a real problem. They just don't have a very strong staff. We had a fellow, Bill Hyland, who spent his career in the CIA and State as a Soviet expert and still writes extensively. He is a very able, thoughtful person. Hal Sonenfeldt is a Soviet expert who also came to the NSC from a long career in State and the CIA. Hal Saunders is still one of our top experts on the Middle East. Bill Quandt was an academic who had been teaching at the University of Pennsylvania. He came to the staff as a Council on Foreign Relations Fellow and stayed. There was a whole group like that, people who came out of the bureaucracy and knew their way around. They had spent their lives, their careers, worrying about these kinds of issues. They could tap into the experts out there who understood these complex issues and could make sure they weren't ignored.

*Question:* I just want to say that this centralization and complexity has an exact parallel in business since World War II with the rise of the conglomerates and R&D (Research and

Development). More complex technology, more product diversity has required more centralization and new organization devices and in R&D this has particularly resulted in the development of the project organization where you have people who follow each project through all the complex designing phases, which was not true beforehand.

*Mr. Odeen:* Yes, there clearly are parallels but on the other hand there are contrary examples, too. I'm sure a lot of you read the book, *In Search of Excellence.* It gives a lot of examples of large and successful conglomerates that have managed to stay decentralized. At 3M whenever a product line gets up to thirty, forty, fifty million dollars in volume they break it up or spin off a piece of it to keep the groups small, more entrepreneurial and manageable. A lot of large, successful corporations have not gone that way. Some of the conglomerates that have developed very rigorous, centralized controls have been less successful.

*Question:* That's not true of R&D. In research and development the project organizations superimpose over the line organization because of the complexity of the design and the interdependence of a great number of technical specialists.

*Mr. Odeen:* The whole question of centralization is one of the key issues in managing our government right now. We've had this steady move toward more and more centralization and pressures for more and better controls. Congress gets into much more detail in terms of program management; they keep asking questions, demanding this and that which tends to force the agency heads to get into that kind of detail as well. I was at a meeting yesterday where we were discussing the federal personnel system. Federal personnel rules and regulations run in excess of 8,000 pages. There is no way anybody can use something like that. All that does is cripple everything or provide a way around everything. But it's an example of the reactions to pressure. Some problem arises and so what do you do? You impose another regulation, another requirement, another report or another rule. Management gets more and more complex. This is a central problem in the administration of the federal government at this time. How do we somehow break this logjam, stop this continued move toward centralization and give people some flexibility to manage and run things?

*Question:* In R&D the project managers are not a central control in the sense that they can tell the line people what to do because they work together so you get a relatively decentralized system with closer control.

*Narrator:* Mr. Odeen has confirmed two propositions of two very wise figures. I've often said that if I were giving a course on national security policy, I would conduct the seminar throughout the semester simply using the Odeen Report because it is a real textbook for how the process works. He confirms also David Broder's comment. David Broder said that he thought the single greatest tragedy in Washington was that we were using about three percent of what he called "centrist resources," moderate people. He mentioned the chairman of the Council of the Miller Center; he mentioned a number of examples in Democratic administrations where moderate people for some reason or another had not been called on. But today we have had a good example of how someone who has served in successive administrations, including Republican administrations, remains an enormous resource if someone found a way to draw on that in the present administration. We have benefited here from his counsel. We would hope that in the months and years ahead that successive administrations in Washington might draw upon his wise outlook on world affairs. Thank you.

PART THREE

# Determining the Threat, Building National Defense

# Discourse on the Threat: National Defense*

JAMES R. SCHLESINGER

*M*r. *Palmer:* On behalf of the trustees, staff, and the spirit of Mr. Jefferson, welcome to Monticello. It is always a pleasure to work with the Miller Center on such a tremendous project as the study of the presidency. You all know its director, Ken Thompson.

*Mr. Thompson:* James Schlesinger was born in New York; he received his A.B. in 1950 from the Virginia of the North, Harvard University; he went on to gain his M.A. in 1952 and his Ph.D. in 1956. He joined the University of Virginia economics faculty in 1956 serving here until 1963. So this is a homecoming for him and a very welcome opportunity for us to have him here. As many of you know he was a senior scholar then Director of Strategic Studies at the Rand Corporation. He went on to become first assistant, then acting deputy director of the Bureau of the Budget, then subsequently assistant director of the Office of Management and the Budget. He served as chairman of the Atomic Energy Commission from 1971 to 1973; he became director of the Central Intelligence Agency; he was secretary of defense from 1973 to 1975. He then was briefly scholar-in-residence at the Johns Hopkins School for Advanced International Studies. He was one of the people whom President Carter turned to early in his campaign and a close rapport developed between them during their early conversations prior to the election. Subsequently he became a special assistant to President Carter. He continued to serve in that capacity until he became the first secretary of the Department of Energy. In 1979 he returned to the private sector to become senior adviser of Lehman Brothers, Kuhn and Loeb; he has had a very active life in Washington since that time in various centers of international studies. He is called on to consult

*Presented at Monticello on July 19, 1984.

**81**

on matters of defense, intelligence, and foreign policy. We are privileged to have a Conversation at Monticello with a former University of Virginia professor.

*Mr. Schlesinger:* I am delighted to be back in Charlottesville as a guest of the Thomas Jefferson Memorial Foundation and the Miller Center and particularly here at Monticello, which I came to know so well as my wife and I escorted visiting firemen around Charlottesville. Monticello was always the first port of call. I frequently pondered how it might have been living with Mr. Jefferson. I think that it must have been rather difficult for his wife. Take the day that he cut the hole in the floor for his grand experiment with the clock. I can well imagine Mrs. Jefferson saying to a servant, "Where is the master?" What must have been her reaction to the response: "Why, Ma'am, he's boring a hole in the living room floor."

When I come out to Monticello I also think of that wonderful vignette which appeared in the *Daily Progress* sometime during the 1950s. At that time there was an ongoing debate whether or not a carillon should be installed in the Chapel on the University grounds. The Chapel had been built long after the Founder's death, but in that letter to the *Daily Progress* an indignant writer stated with great finality: "If Mr. Jefferson had intended that there be a carillon in the Chapel, he would have left suitable instructions in his will."

Jefferson, of course, appreciated the need for change. I throw that out as an initial observation just before we get into the Conversation. That will concern the changing international position of the United States and the inevitable consequences such change will have for the conduct of our foreign policy.

If we cast our minds back to 1945, the United States at that time was the preponderant power in the world. In addition to a monopoly of nuclear weapons, it had some sixty percent of the world's manufacturing capacity and perhaps half of the world's gross product. Our position of dominance reflected the simple fact that this nation alone had emerged from World War II undamaged. The American public's attitude today still reflects that 20 year period after World War II when the United States was militarily the preponderant power in the world. It was thus a period in which American actions could be decisive even when it acted belatedly.

I stress the need to accept change. In the course of the last twenty years there has been an erosion of the American position, some of it a reflection of our own inadequacies, but much of it inevitable. For example, the American share of the world product has now declined from fifty percent to perhaps twenty percent. Today we are under pressure from competitors, perhaps most notably from some of our former enemies. The decline of the American position has also reflected the internal discontents that flowed from disputes over our role in the Vietnam War. But the thing we have to bear in mind today is that the position of the United States is no longer invulnerable. Its word therefore can no longer be decisive.

In Europe today there is concern about American behavior to an extent that simply did not exist in the 1940s or 1950s. In those days the United States could readily be considered the Great Protector of Europe while effectively precluding any external threat to the European states. Indeed, there was little effort on their part.

In the 1980s there has been growing concern regarding America's role in the Third World and the fear that that role will feed back into Europe, causing an erosion of Europe's relations with the East. That concern may be justified or not. It may be rational or irrational. But it is there, and it is something that we shall have to deal with.

In the 1980s the United States to some extent, and even more notably the allies of the United States, are dependent upon the oil resources of the Persian Gulf. That region of the world is one in which the United States throughout the fifties and the sixties was the preponderant power. Today, to illustrate the change, a war has rolled on for four years between Iran and Iraq with potentially serious consequences for us. Yet the United States, formerly the most influential power in the region, maintains diplomatic relations with neither.

Now I stress this fundamental change in our position because it is something that we shall have to live with and adapt to. Yet, the expectations and the aspirations of the American public are to a large extent based upon that earlier (and indeed happier day) when the United States was the world's preponderant power. The American public is not used to reversals. At the same time, it is not used to the high costs of involvement in foreign policy.

Today the net advantages in military position may lie, not with the United States, but with the Soviet Union. Happily, the Soviet Union has been a very cautious and conservative power. Someday it may change. For the moment, however, it remains a very cautious power. Therefore one need not expect significant troubles simply because of the alteration of the military balance.

Over the course of the decades ahead we shall to a large extent have to substitute astuteness, cleverness, and the use of diplomatic and economic tools for sheer military strength. In the past we did not have to use such tools extensively in light of our great military advantages.

In the period ahead the United States must behave with circumspection, understanding the concerns of others—and most notably those of our European allies.

This altered international position coincides with a period of domestic change that has come since the Vietnam War. That includes the re-assertion of congressional power. The irony is that at a time when we need greater domestic consensus to sustain our foreign policy in a period inherently more difficult than that of the forties and fifties, our domestic consensus has broken down. We no longer have what we had in earlier periods: immediate, instinctive public support for the president on foreign policy matters—for any president! We no longer have the willingness of the Congress to defer to presidential leadership.

Now, ladies and gentlemen, I am optimistic that we shall be able to move satisfactorily through this period of change and that we shall be able to adjust to our reduced power and to understand the changes that are inevitable. For the American position, once preponderant, is now "merely" that of leading power in the world—*primus inter pares* amongst its allies, but no longer the dominant power.

Let me simply throw these thoughts out as my initial observations. Note that I have started with Jefferson's belief in embracing change, be it in the vestibule at Monticello, the carillon in the chapel, or in the larger context of American foreign policy.

*Question:* Mr. Secretary, you've dealt with the national military establishment. Do you think the civilian control over the inter-service rivalry is sufficient to approve their consumption of our resources to the extent the military budget is now taking?

*Mr. Schlesinger:* Your question is a good statement of the problem. Briefly the answer is no. The degree of control has diminished in recent years. In the years that I was secretary of defense, I had the great advantage, in a sense, that the reputation of the Pentagon and the military services had sunk so low on Capitol Hill that there was no way that a service could get a program adopted without coming through the office of the secretary of defense.

Today among the many advantages of the restoration of the prestige of the military is the disadvantage that they are no longer constrained to come through that office. And the desire of the office of the secretary of defense to impose control over the services has also diminished. That seems to me unfortunate. One must force, in order to make the best use of our resources, the services to work cooperatively. If they do not work cooperatively each service will emphasize that mission that uniquely reflects its institutional self-image. The Air Force will be less concerned with providing air cover for the Army than with improving its capabilities for deep interdiction. The Navy, never particularly fond of working with the other services, will be floating more and more aircraft carriers—for that is the mission closest to the Navy's heart. And the Army will be attempting to compensate for the assignment of air cover to the Air Force through the purchase of costly attack helicopters. Moreover, one should pressure the services to cooperate in their procurement practices.

There is another aspect to the resource problem. If we go back to that period of the fifties and sixties in which the United States utterly dominated the world militarily, we did not then have to worry about the system of command within the military establishment. We were able, after World War II, to move partly toward unification, yet, nonetheless, to preserve all of the prerogatives of the military services. The result is that we now have a JCS system that is the Achilles' heel in the process of military planning. Normally each of the chiefs will have to vote in favor of a proposal to achieve the sought-after unanimity. Unanimity is, of course, like the old Polish veto. It means that each of the services can effectively block a proposal. The upshot is that we are not getting appropriate professional advice from our military people. It is time that we give up the post-World War II fear that an effective military advisory system, cutting across service lines, would somehow or other move us in the direction of a Prussian General Staff. That professional body was mistakenly believed to be responsible somehow or other for Hitler's policies in Europe during the late thirties and early forties.

We no longer have the resources to squander in pursuit of the separate ambitions of four military services: We should create a planning process that makes most effective use of the assets of all the Services.

*Question:* You served on the Scowcroft Commission in this administration. What should the Congress do about the MX and what are they likely to do about the MX?

*Mr. Schlesinger:* The Congress should continue to vote money for the production of the MX.

I am less concerned with the precise rate of production than I am to maintain an open production line. The MX is important in relation to our bargaining position vis-à-vis the Soviets in any arms control negotiations. If the Congress were to kill off the MX, that would remove one of the incentives for the Soviets to negotiate seriously. The MX is also important in terms of alliance strategy. The United States is committed to use its strategic forces in support of Western Europe if it is massively attacked by the conventional forces of the Warsaw Pact. The likelihood of that occurring is very low, but the reason the likelihood is low is that we have maintained a plausible deterrent over the years. I think that the MX is an important element of that deterrent.

An underlying problem for the MX is that the Congress has mistrusted President Reagan's views on arms control. To save the MX the administration will have to remain credible in its arms control position. Moreover, as all of you have noted, the nation has run into a considerable budget problem with deficits approaching two hundred billion dollars a year. Over the course of this decade I believe the deficit is more likely to reach 300 billion dollars a year than to fall to 125 billion dollars.

Thus, the Congress is eager to cut defense spending for purely budgetary reasons and, simultaneously, it is also anxious to express its skepticism about the President's commitment to arms control. The MX now hangs by a thread. The latest vote in the Senate, which has been the body more favorable to the MX, was 48 to 48, broken by a vote of the vice president. Unless we have a change in attitude I doubt that the MX will survive through next year. It will, however, be all right for this year.

All this is a reflection of a tendency that has emerged since Vietnam and the Watergate episode for Congress to feel, not only free to challenge a President's position, but an obligation to do so. The MX has been supported by the Nixon, Ford, Carter and Reagan administrations. It has the support of the overwhelming number of people who have been in senior positions in national security affairs. Nonetheless, despite all of what would previously have been regarded as excellent credentials for a favorable vote, the MX hangs by a thread and is unlikely to survive next year in the Congress unless there is a change in attitude.

*Question:* In regard to the MX, how much serious consideration was given to an alternate system that was addressed essentially to the problem of vulnerability as opposed to the problem of first-strike capability? Is it really infeasible for us to have a system that would either be put on small submarines or small mobile craft that would move around rather than putting something like the MX out there in those holes that are just as vulnerable no matter how big the missile is?

*Mr. Schlesinger:* No, it is not impossible. Your question goes to the very heart of the political difficulties that we have had. President Carter authorized the MX system. Incidentally we should also recall that in his inaugural address President Carter stated as his goal to expunge nuclear weapons from the face of the earth. Yet, by the time he had been in office three years, he was prepared to authorize the MX system. That suggests the very powerful national security reasons for approving the MX. But he also proposed a very complex basing system which included, as things would have it, deployment in the states of Nevada and Utah. The senators from Nevada and Utah were prominent in conservative Republican circles and rather prominent among the incoming President's friends.

Partly to eliminate any contamination from the Carter deployment scheme, partly to ease the political pressures in those two states, the original MX deployment scheme was scrapped. That may not have been a weapons-system mistake but it surely was a political mistake. What the administration should have done in my judgment was simply to say: we are not enthused about the Carter deployment proposal. Nonetheless, we do have an ongoing program and therefore we will proceed with Carter's scheme. Instead the administration fell back. It took almost two years to make a decision with regard to deployment. The current deployment proposal incidentally does not achieve what the President stated repeatedly in the campaign was his objective: to close the so-called window of vulnerability. It has thus created political vulnerabilities of its own.

I believe that in the Scowcroft recommendations we should have placed more stress on alternative basing modes after the initial deployment in the Minuteman holes. It was necessary to get the system started and the only place to put the missiles quickly was in the holes. But one of the alternatives we should be considering is submersible barges that could move around the coastal fringes of the United States or the Great Lakes. These could be relatively invulnerable. It would thus reduce Soviet confidence that they could target such missiles. So I think that we should still be looking for a more suitable alternative.

Finally, perhaps what is more important, we have concentrated too much on vulnerability of silos. The President himself has contributed significantly to this focus on silo vulnerability as the principal element in considering deployment of a new intercontinental ballistic missile. Nonetheless, we should bear in mind that the vulnerability that must concern us is the *overall* vulnerability of the deterrent. The role for the MX missile is to provide a threat against *Soviet* ICBMs in the event that the Warsaw Pact was to move against Western Europe. It helps shore up deterrence of an assault against Western Europe. However improbable nuclear war is, the most likely way that nuclear war could get started is still a conventional assault against Western Europe. By contrast, the likelihood of a Soviet bolt from the blue, a nuclear Pearl Harbor, is very low simply because the Soviet leaders have been rational, very rational and very cautious in that respect.

*Question:* I asked the question because another former University of Virginia professor who is now the head of strategic studies at the Naval War College also came to give a talk. When we were debating this very subject I asked him the question of whether the Navy really gave any serious study to the kind of system you were suggesting. He said absolutely not. And I began to wonder if the mythology of the triad with the service connections thereto was inhibiting the research into that very system.

*Mr. Schlesinger:* The mythology of the triad, no, but interservice deference, yes. The Navy wants to get along with the Air Force. Until you get a real budget crunch you are not going to have naval officers slipping up to Capitol Hill and attacking the MX directly. The Air Force will defer to the Navy and the Navy will defer to the Air Force until there is a real budget crunch. Then we are likely to have a return to interservice rivalry of the most ugly variety. Nonetheless, the Air Force was encouraged during the 1960s to look at such submersibles. Among others it was encouraged by the Rand Corporation. That perhaps is why I have some nostalgia for the barge concept. The reaction of the Air Force was basically institutional: a submersible means deployment in water and water is the Navy's medium. If we deploy the MX in water then the Navy is likely to get hold of the program and we're not going to run that risk. We prefer to accept the risks from the Soviets.

*Question:* With all the protection that the modern carrier force has, will the carriers survive attack?

*Mr. Schlesinger:* The large carrier is probably survivable so long as it does not go into the highest threat areas. There has been some talk—and I think rather loose talk—about steaming carriers off Murmansk or Vladivostok. If they go into such high threat areas I would not give much chance for their survival. But in lower intensity conflict they probably remain survivable. A harder question is: when they have suffered *some* damage under attack, can they still be effectively employed? And that's an unanswered question. A still harder question is what about the future? What happens, for example, when the Soviets follow the Americans, fifteen or twenty years out, and they get Stealth technology which they use on their air-to-surface missiles? Under those circumstances our ability to detect missiles would be no greater than, let us say, the ability of the British forces in the Falkland Islands to detect Exocet missiles. That would surely raise a question about either survivability or the effectiveness of the carriers at that later date.

My own view is that we are now probably over-investing in carrier task forces. I would certainly like to have more carriers if they were lower in cost. With a budget that is being squeezed, I would probably prefer to invest in other capabilities.

*Question:* Mr. Secretary, would you say something about what Mondale would look like in that security policy book in substance and style?

*Mr. Schlesinger:* Mondale is a very intelligent man. His private behavior is quite different from his public image—which he has been all too effective in creating. His image is of an unusually stolid Norwegian who rarely smiles and certainly has no sense of humor. Yet, in reality, he has a splendid sense of humor and a very light touch. And as I say, he is quite intelligent. On many issues of domestic policy, including, perhaps surprisingly, on budget issues, I would think that he could be an effective decision-maker. Whether or not he could persuade the Congress as effectively as President Reagan is another question. Reagan's substantive knowledge is far, far less about many of these issues than is Mondale's, but Reagan's leadership skills are substantial and the capacity to lead is increasingly important in a president. Oddly enough, I would have relatively little concern about Mondale on domestic issues. I would have a great deal of concern about him on foreign policy issues. The reason I would have that concern is that despite his intelligence there remains some question about his toughness. Now this is almost a technical observation: presidents just require backbone. Some have it and some don't. And you can't blame those who don't have it.

Whatever his disadvantages with regard to the subtleties of diplomacy, Reagan has that capacity. In four years he has established a worldwide belief that Ronald Reagan is not a man to be trifled with. In foreign policy, that is immensely important. Given Mondale's amiability, which is substantial, and his intelligence it's not clear to me that he would be able to sustain the prevailing belief in other countries that you don't fiddle around with the United States.

Now I would also be concerned about the nature of the advice that Mondale would receive on foreign policy problems and I would be concerned about the influence of Jesse Jackson on the Democratic Party. Jackson has become, in effect, a spokesman for the Third World, reflected in his recent visit to Central America and to Cuba. I do not find it altogether reassuring, as reported, that Mr. Jackson can shout in Cuba, "Viva Che Guevara!" I find it even more disturbing that no senior personage in the Democratic Party has said, "Hey, we can't have that." There is a real question about the future effectiveness of the Democratic Party on foreign policy issues. This may be overridden through the strength of particular personalities or through greater concern with domestic issues, but there is, I believe, that difficult question.

*Question:* Would you couple that with a comment about the future, if it has one, of the Jackson wing of the Democratic Party?

*Mr. Schlesinger:* You are referring here, I take it, not to Jesse Jackson but to the late Henry M. Jackson. The American public is normally in the middle of the road, perhaps especially so now. The Democratic Party had a chance to get back into the middle of the road. Partly because the centrist candidates—the Hollingses and the Glenns—fell out relatively early, the debate in the Democratic Party has taken place essentially on the left, with the former vice president being clearly the most conservative of the three candidates. There was no attempt in San Francisco to throw even a small bone to the Jackson wing of the party. On defense issues, the Jackson wing is represented by the so-called Coalition For A Democratic Majority, which suggested some planks on defense issues. It would have been relatively easy to incorporate some of those planks and some of their language just to say we are taking care of *all* elements in the party. That was not done. That does not bode well, at least in the short term, for the Jackson wing of the party.

*Question:* Mr. Secretary, could you discuss a little the issue about the continuing budget deficit, its consequences, what

should be done about it, what will be done about it under either of
the two administrations?

*Mr. Schlesinger:* The budget deficit may become an increasingly difficult problem. You are all aware of the consequences of a
budget deficit that runs five or six percent of the gross national
product in a society which has a very low rate of personal savings
for an advanced democracy. Personal savings in the United
States is about five percent of the GNP. In Canada it is about
thirteen percent of the GNP; in Japan it is about twenty-five
percent. So we have fewer resources for investment coming from
savings. We cannot afford to fritter away that limited resource on
financing federal deficits. Nonetheless, we now have an immense
deficit—partly reflecting ideological convictions at the onset of
the administration that somehow or other cutting tax rates was
going to bring about a balanced budget. The supply-side belief
was tested that tax cuts would lead to an explosion of effort on
the part of countless citizens and thus an increase in tax reve-
nues. Quite clearly that has not happened. One danger in the
present fiscal situation may be that the longer it drags on the more
politically acceptable it becomes.

As an analogue, I have used an episode that occurred in
Geneva in 1935, when Mussolini invaded Abyssinia. The League
of Nations wanted to demonstrate that it could effectively handle
this threat to international peace. Discussions continued
endlessly at the League's headquarters in Geneva. At the close of
each day's deliberations there was a briefing for the press. At the
end of one of the many press briefings, one of the journalists
observed, "On the surface very little is happening, but beneath
the surface *nothing* is happening."

That little episode tells you a great deal about the questions of
the deficit.

Just in this last year interest rates have climbed about two
percent and that has added about $25 million to the cost of
servicing the debt. At the same time that we are getting this surge
in interest payments, we are chipping away at certain non-
defense expenditures of the federal government. But the longer
this immense deficit continues, the higher go our interest payments—about $20 billion a year. They grow more surely than we
can chip away at other government expenditures.

If you look at the President's Program for Economic Recovery that was published in February of 1981, it projected that interest payments in 1989 would be less than one percent of the gross national product. In fact, by 1989 such payments will be about four percent of the gross national product—almost twenty percent of total federal outlays. So we are losing ground the longer we defer action.

My greatest fear is that the passage of time will tend to make the problem worse. Politically it will make it worse because it may legitimize deficits of this magnitude. Italy, for example, runs a deficit equal to about fifteen percent of the gross national product. The reaction is: Who cares? But ours is a different kind of society. It is also a society that happens to be the international banker. It is very important that *we* not run deficits of this magnitude.

Nonetheless, the passage of time does legitimize these deficits. The great worry is that Ronald Reagan may be the man who gives them legitimacy. One can, I believe, say this with assurance. If one has a Ted Kennedy as President of the United States in 1989 or 1993, given *his* views on these matters, he is not likely to fight to reduce the federal deficit to levels below those that were acceptable to Ronald Reagan. Just the fact that Ronald Reagan has accepted deficits of this size without seriously fighting them may serve to make them permanent.

Therein lies my deepest concern. Yes, we ought to solve that problem. And the way that we should solve that problem is quite simple, though painful—pay higher taxes, not necessarily equal to the total size of the deficit, but approximately half of that deficit. There is simply no way that we are going to cut federal expenditures by as much as one hundred billion dollars. We shall have to accept that a substantial part of the deficit problem cannot be solved through a reduction of government activities, but can only be solved by paying higher taxes.

Part of our problem in the course of the last decade—and one of those changes that Mr. Jefferson might especially have noted— is the declining willingness of the public to pay taxes. Nobody likes to pay taxes. Yet, if we are going to solve the deficit problem we must rid ourselves of illusions—either the more extreme versions of supply-side economics or the Proposition 13 mentality that somehow or other one can squeeze expenditures simply by reducing the tax base.

I worried about these problems when I was in the Bureau of

the Budget. Even then one could foresee the surge of social and economic expendidtures creating a future problem in relation to the fiscal capacity of the United States. But that surge has now occurred. There is no way for us radically to reduce the entitlements programs going to the American public. We may slow somewhat the rate of growth. Indeed, we are having some success. But that is not a *reduction*. That means for at least the next four or five years, probably the next decade, the only way to deal with a substantial part of the deficit is through an increase in taxes. I do hope that the administration will turn in that direction after the election. But there has been a good deal of doubt on that score, and the administration's objectives certainly are not clear. To this point the President has repeatedly said that he will veto *any* tax increase. He clearly regards the reduction in income taxes as the central accomplishment of his administration.

There is no way to get a tax increase in this country unless the President is out in front. You asked earlier about congressional attitudes. Perhaps the wisest, if somewhat cynical reporter in Washington, the late Peter Lisagor of the *Chicago News,* once said that it is easy to predict what Congress will do. Just think of the cowardly thing to do—and that's precisely what Congress will do.

To raise taxes you will have to get the President out in front. The Republican leadership of the Senate has been very imaginative and courageous on this issue, not only the leader, Howard Baker, but Pete Domenici and Bob Dole as well. About nine months ago Dole, steadily pursued by worried people from the financial community as well as by the press, commented in a private gathering, "If anyone thinks that Rostenkowski and I are going to alienate our constituents by pressing for a tax increase and then have that tax increase vetoed, leaving us with the responsibility of dealing not only with our constituents, but our colleagues in the House and the Senate who have run political risks by voting for tax increases, they are simply not living in the real world." Once again, you have to get the President out in front. Otherwise there is no way, given public attitudes, that you could get a tax increase, no matter how courageous individual senators may be. The President will have to turn around.

Whatever concerns one may have about Mondale's strength in foreign policy, the Democrats will be far more willing and, there are those who believe, eager to raise taxes. The question is not their reluctance in that area. The question is what will be associated with that increase in taxes? Will it be a further increase in the domestic programs that have been the source of these difficulties or will it be a reduction in the deficit? That too is an unanswered question.

I should also add partly in response to the prior question that Mr. Mondale is not an ideologue on these issues. He is quite different from, say, Senator Kennedy. And he is quite rational on these matters. He may indeed be what Republicans describe as a "bleeding heart", but on many issues he is neither ideological nor very far left. I think that he would be a far more prudent president on domestic affairs than his background in the Democratic Party and the Farmer-Labor Party might suggest. He has certainly recognized the change in public sentiment in this country and the change that has come about in our fiscal capacity.

Notice, this is the first Democratic platform in twenty-odd years that does not propose a national medical plan. It is the first Democratic platform in several decades, probably in four or five decades, that does not propose a host of new domestic initiatives. I think that reflects the fact that at least the Mondale people recognize the fiscal cupboard is pretty bare.

*Question:* Mr. Secretary, Peter Grace spoke to us several weeks ago here. Do you care to comment on his report?

*Mr. Schlesinger:* Sure. Many of these reports are made more for reasons of public imagery than with any serious hope of substantial accomplishment in the Congress.

There is an old story about a farmer who was told by the agricultural extension agent that he could teach him improved techniques that would permit him to double his production. "Hell," observed this farmer, "I already know how to farm twice as well as I'm presently doing." Sometimes additional instruction is superfluous.

Something like that is appropriate with respect to the Grace Commission findings. It is always good to be reminded that there is a lot of pork in the defense establishment and that there are many programs that have no strong economic justification. However when you see a program that lacks strong economic justification, you can be well assured that those on Capitol Hill probably recognize that, too. The reason that you have the program is not because of a strong economic justification but a powerful political constituency behind the program that is not going to be denied. And no President can take on too many political constituencies. So these areas for potential savings are far easier to point out than to get enacted by the Congress or indeed even by the executive branch.

There is another matter. While some of the savings in the Grace Commission report did indeed involve areas of great inefficiency, the majority of the savings came from recommendations for changes in policy. It was less a question of getting the government to do something more efficiently than to get the government out of certain lines of activity. Thus, it becomes not an argument about government efficiency, but an argument about the appropriate range of government activities. While one may feel very strongly that the government should not be underwriting the deficit of the postal system or giving aid to the handicapped, that does not mean that the American people similarly regard these as inappropriate federal activities. Moreover, the fact that the federal government has undertaken such functions, suggests once again that there are significant pressures to do just that.

Inertia may be the most important element in determining the shape of future government expenditures. The Grace Commission is useful in challenging the prevailing inertia but it disregards—as perhaps it should—all these little pockets of political powers that are sustained by government programs. And it diverges rather sharply from what is clearly the majority view of the U.S. public regarding the appropriate range of federal activity. Consequently, I doubt that you will see many of the recommendations actually implemented.

*Question:* To go back to your point about our reduced economic role in the world—from some fifty percent to twenty percent—we have to take into account the interests and wishes of our allies more. To what extent do you think we are going to be successful in getting the European allies and Britain to take on more responsibility for the defense of Europe and the forward defense?

*Mr. Schlesinger:* I think that the chances are close to zero. There will be a great deal of talk about significantly improving the conventional forces in Europe, but there has been substantial talk about that ever since the 1950s. Indeed it has been American policy since the Kennedy administration came into power, just after the time General Maxwell Taylor published *The Uncertain Trumpet.* The threat of nuclear retaliation as a deterrent has over time diminished in credibility, as the Soviets have built up their counter-deterrence and the corresponding need for more conventional forces was anticipated.

The basic problem is that the Europeans have a different assessment of the Soviet threat from the Americans. The irony is that the Americans take the security of Europe far more seriously than do the Europeans themselves. The European view is, with some justification by the way, that the Americans are too excited about the Soviets. They think we regard the Soviets as far more belligerent and menacing than the Soviets actually are. They have lived on the same continent with the Russian people for generations. They strongly believe that, while the Soviets must be considered as a threat, they are not going to invade Western Europe unless they are given a welcome opportunity. There is a good deal of truth in that assessment, particularly with regard to Western Europe. Whether or not the European assessment of the Soviet problem in the Horn of Africa or in the Middle East is as perceptive is an open question.

The Americans historically have worried about increasing conventional forces and making the conventional deterrent a more impressive part of the overall NATO deterrent. The Europeans have not thought that to be as necessary as the Americans. And since the costs of a conventional deterrent fall on the Europeans, as opposed to the nuclear deterrent falling on the Americans, they have been satisfied with the present situation. They have been prepared in dealing with the Soviet threat to accept a low-confidence deterrent. By contrast, the Americans have over the years insisted on a high-confidence deterrent.

I didn't think there was much chance of the Europeans doing substantially more in convential forces even in earlier periods. But now they have serious economic problems. My conclusion is I would not waste too much American political capital in fruitless preaching at the Europeans about the advantages of improved conventional defenses in Europe. The Americans keep thinking that the reason the Europeans have not responded is that they didn't understand what we were saying. The fact is the Europeans have clearly understood what we have been saying. They simply disagree with our assessment of the threat, and they probably lack the political capability to increase defense expenditures very much, even if they did agree with our assessment. So I expect to see a great deal more talk and remarkably little action.

*Question:* Sir, what do you think of President Reagan's support for star wars technology?

*Mr. Schlesinger:* I myself thought that the announcement in the President's speech of March of last year was unwise. Even if we were prepared to do the research and development which to a large extent we are, the issue should not have been raised to that degree of public prominence. It frightened the Europeans and they are still frightened. It fed the Soviet paranoia. The Soviets believe that the Reagan administration is attempting to restore the period of American preponderance. I would like very much to see that occur, but it is just not feasible. But the Russians fear just that. They say that the strategic arms program, the specific proposals of START, and the Strategic Defense Initiative (so-called Star Wars) are all intended to restore American strategic dominance.

I would have preferred not to have fed those Soviet fears. I also think that it is probably ill-advised to feed the hopes of the U.S. public. We are going to have to live throughout our lifetimes with the capacity of the Soviet Union to destroy the cities of the United States. Star Wars, even if it can reduce the weight of the Soviet attack, can not preclude Soviet attack against American cities and that is the hope that the President originally held out. However that is water over the dam. Whether or not he should have said it, he said it. And therefore, in my judgment, we ought to attempt to exploit it.

One of the things about the Soviet Union is that they are drawn into strategic arms discussions primarily by the bait of being able to head off an American program. We should be prepared in the 1980s, just as President Nixon was prepared in

1972, to tie together offensive and defensive weapons. Logically they are tied together. In 1972 Nixon said to the Soviets, who didn't want to sign the strategic arms limitation agreement, "If you don't sign a SALT agreement, we're not going to have the ABM Treaty." The Soviets were prepared to accept the limit on strategic offensive forces to get the agreement on defensive systems in which they feared that the Americans were far ahead of them. I think we should be prepared to do exactly the same thing with regard to these proposals for space defense.

What I suspect will happen in Vienna, if Vienna indeed takes place, is that the Soviet Union, which changes its policies very slowly—we may be too mercurial ourselves, but their policies are based on inertia—will just continue to use that forum through the election for propaganda. After the election it is possible that we may lure them back for serious discussions. Whatever may be said about the limitations of strategic arms discussions, a seriousness of American intent in this matter is essential both to reassure our allies and to reassure even the American public. No administration can afford to appear cynical about arms control. Even if it harbors private misgivings, it must make every honest effort in this field or it will lose the support of its allies and the American people.

The Reagan administration in its first two years went too far in expressing doubts about arms control. That is one of the reasons that we are having the difficulties in the Congress with respect to the MX. There is great skepticism on the Hill, which I consider unjust, regarding Mr. Reagan's commitment to arms control. After two years in office, partly reflecting the work of the Scowcroft Commission, the President went through some kind of adjustment in his views. He is deeply dedicated to arms control. Nonetheless he does have low credibility on the Hill because of earlier statements of the administration.

*Narrator:* Besides cutting holes in the floor, Mr. Jefferson liked to bring together the most stimulating and provocative minds in his time. We try to do that with these Monticello Conversations, and today has been no exception. Thank you very much, Mr. Schlesinger.

PART FOUR

# Communication Across the Separation of Powers

# Foreign Policy and the Separation of Powers*

DEAN RUSK

*M*r. *Thompson:* I'm pleased to welcome you to ceremonies involved in the third annual Burkett Miller Award. It is my great honor to introduce the recently inaugurated president of the University, Robert Marchant O'Neil.

*President O'Neil:* Thank you, Professor Thompson. It is a particular honor to be able to present the annual Burkett Miller award to Dean Rusk. The selection is amply justified by Mr. Rusk's eminent career as scholar and statesman, and of those qualities I will say more in just a moment.

At the outset, however, I wanted to recall an earlier meeting as evidence of the person we honor this afternoon. It was during one of the tensest times for American diplomacy, the aftermath of the Cuban missile crisis in the fall of 1962, that the U.S. Supreme Court law clerks invited the Secretary of State to be our luncheon guest. Only that brash and self assured group would have had the temerity to extend such an invitation in the first place. Despite all the pressures of the day the Secretary responded quickly and affirmatively. He came to the clerk's luncheon room in the basement of the court and, as I recall, we not only asked him to carry his own tray but to pay for his own lunch. And we then spent the better part of two hours visiting with him, asking difficult and occasionally impertinent but never irrelevant questions on United States foreign policy. He imparted to us a sense of confidence about the destiny of our country at that very critical juncture. None of us who had the great privilege, two of whom are currently law faculty colleagues of mine here, could ever forget our debt to our distinguished visitor. And it is in part for that quite personal reason that I am so pleased to be able to repay in small measure this afternoon.

*Presented in the Dome Room of the Rotunda on October 3, 1985.

This award is fitting, not only because of Mr. Rusk's achievement as scholar and statesman, but also because of the wise counsel and active support that he has given to the work of the Miller Center itself. His help has taken many different forms: he advanced the idea of a Commission of Presidential Transitions and Foreign Policy which the Center then initiated with two of Mr. Rusk's successors, William Rogers and Cyrus Vance, serving as the co-chairs. As early as the 1950s he focused public attention on the problem and possible effects of illness among high public officials and that was the subject of the fourth Miller Center Commission. As a former Rhodes scholar and as president of the Rockefeller Foundation, he wrote and spoke often of the relation of American values to those of other cultures. Decades later, with the help of the Exxon Educational Foundation, the Center launched inquiries which resulted in publication of twenty individual monographs on the projection of American values abroad.

The link between scholarship and leadership in public affairs runs throughout Mr. Rusk's career. When President John Kennedy announced the appointment of his Secretary of State he displayed for the press Mr. Rusk's celebrated foreign affairs article on the presidency and explained the role it had played in the selection. The identification of that article with the Center's primary mission hardly needs elaboration. Later, Mr. Rusk became the first person of national eminence to serve as an Associate of the Miller Center. Soon thereafter, he visited the Center and in a pair of two day meetings he took part in a series of colloquia with faculty, students and community leaders, focusing on and revisiting that memorable foreign affairs article.

While it is the years of public service that deserve and receive national acclaim from our honored guest, we especially honor him as a professor, a role he has held both before and after his time in the national spotlight. The contacts our students and colleagues have had with him have been unfailingly valuable in the best professorial sense. Whether or not the general public fully understands and appreciates it, he has spoken for moderation and restraint on a wide range of issues from U.S. involvement in Southeast Asia to the militarization of outer space. Long before individual Presidents came to adapt tactics and policy to underlying realities in the nuclear age, he cautioned that Americans and Russians must somehow learn to coexist, and if there is one lesson that we took away from our session with him twenty-five years ago, it was, I think, that one. For his humanity and public service, his courage and integrity, his unflinching good spirits in adversity, and his steady focus on the essentials of governance, including the presidency, we are honored to present the Burkett Miller award to the fifty-fourth Secretary of State, Dean Rusk.

*Secretary Rusk:* Thank you very much, President O'Neil, Kenneth Thompson, members and guests of the community of learning of the University of Virginia. I am delighted to be in this historic place, designed, by the way, by the first Secretary of State. I'm deeply complimented by this distinguished award with which you are presenting me today. I especially appreciate, President O'Neil, the generosity of your remarks. Now that I am happily dropping out of the public eye, I don't take introductions for granted anymore. I've now reached the point where people stop me on the streets and in airports, and say, "Haven't I seen you somewhere before?" One of the legendary little old ladies came up to me at the Atlanta Airport some time ago and planted herself firmly about three feet in front of me and said, "You're in television." I said, "Oh, you remember Hoss Cartwright of Bonanza, don't you?" She went away very happy.

I have sometimes been asked what it was like to make the transition from the excitement and drama of the official position in Washington back to the quiet groves of academe. I've usually referred to the exhilaration which one feels in being relieved of such responsibilities and the joy of becoming a private citizen again. For example, I've recaptured my right of free speech, including the right of silence. But there has been one problem. I was trained by people like Harry Truman and George Marshall and many a congressional committee and many a press conference to say what I had to say as briefly as possible and then shut up. When I got back to the campus I found that whatever it was I wanted to say was supposed to last for fifty minutes. I'm not going to do that to you this afternoon. I want to get to your questions before we adjourn. I will speak impressionistically, leaving it to you to complete many of the paragraphs in your own way. If these remarks are to be published in any way, I beg the congressional privilege of revising and extending my remarks in the record.

*The separation of powers and the conduct of our foreign relations.* Whatever theorists may have to say about it, the separation of powers is real. It is a fundamental part of our constitutional system and it gives rise to constitutional tensions throughout the day on every working day throughout the year.

Chief Justice Earl Warren visited our Law School shortly before his death and on that occasion reminded us that if each branch of the federal government were to pursue its own constitutional powers to the end of the trail our system simply could not function. In effect he was saying that it would freeze up like an engine without oil. Impasse is the overhanging threat in our constitutional system, deliberately made complicated by our Founding Fathers in order to place restraints upon the exercise of the raw power of government. We sometimes forget that our own constitutional history merges with that of England in the latter part of the eighteenth century.

One of the moments I deeply cherish was the privilege I had in 1965 of going to Runnymede, the field of Magna Carta, and there receiving from Her Majesty the Queen, an acre of ground at Runnymede as a gift from the British people to the American people in memory of John F. Kennedy. I thought some of you might be intrigued with the thought that you own a little piece of Runnymede. But it was a reminder that not only Magna Carta but the petition of right, the Habeas Corpus Act and the English Bill of Rights were part of our own constitutional history. That includes some of those old common law judges, who at the risk of their own lives, over against the crown and sometimes the parliament, would put their arms around a prisoner at the bar and say, "You cannot do this to this man."

The result of moving that constitutional history one step further has been to give us a written constitution, enforceable by the courts in important respects over against both the executive and legislative power; a system which enshrines, if I may speak metaphorically, the notion, the old common law notion, that the King can do no wrong, transforming it into the notion that if it is wrong, the King must not be permitted to do it.

The first sentence of Article I of the Constitution reads, "all legislative powers herein granted shall be vested in the Congress of the United States . . . ." The first sentence of Article II says, "The Executive power shall be vested in a President of the United States of America." Now there have been times in the past when scholars have tried to derive special meaning from that phrase in Article I, "herein granted," as a most severe limitation upon legislative power than one finds in the delegation of executive power to the president. But over the passage of time my own impression is that any possible distinction derived from those words is more or less meaningless.

There is a good deal of literature about the extraordinary increase in the powers of the presidency. Some of it, in my judgment, is somewhat exaggerated. There is less literature on the extraordinary increase in the powers of the Congress: the extension of the notion of interstate and foreign commerce, the use of Section V of Article XIV to enforce such notions as the equal protection of the laws building upon the general welfare clause in the Preamble to the Constitution and by its power to tax and to spend. The Congress has over the years bought from the states considerable constitutional power by saying to the states, "Now here is some money and you can have some of it if you will accept our guidelines as to how you use it." States, often in fiscal disarray, have not been reluctant to come forward and take that money in exchange for surrender of some of their authority.

Another channel by which congressional power has been increased comes through the oversight function. Just in the last twenty years, the oversight function has exploded. Almost everything that the executive branch does is subject to inquiry by a committee or subcommittee of the Congress in some sort of fashion resulting, in my judgment, in a considerable intrusion into proper executive functions.

Then there is the General Accounting Office, the GAO. In my day the GAO was made up of a group of auditors. Their job was to see to it that funds spent by the government were covered by appropriate appropriations bills, and that any expenditures beyond those bills had to be somehow repaired. But if you look at the monthly reports prepared by the General Accounting Office in the last ten to fifteen years, you will see that that agency, which is an arm of Congress, has been making evaluative studies of all sorts of policy questions for which the GAO has no responsibility. I have not been able to ascertain in what way the Congress exerecises supervision over the GAO. Any member of Congress, House or Senate, can ask the GAO for a study, and unless there are very strong reasons why the GAO cannot make that study, they will proceed with it. If they themselves do not have in-house staff with the time and the competence to make a particular study they will go out and hire outsiders to come in and make the study for them. There is some danger that the GAO is becoming an uncontrolled fourth branch of the government by the extension of its investigative and reporting capabilities.

One small team of GAO investigators went out to the Strategic Air Command Headquarters in the midwest and demanded from the commanding general that he turn over to them a complete set of targeting plans for our nuclear warheads. Fortunately, the general refused. But in any event, there again is an extension of the power of the Congress.

The phrase, "the executive power," is not defined in the Constitution. There are some executive functions which are spelled out in the text of the Constitution itself. But there have been those who claim that the phrase "the executive power" is itself, an independent grant of power to the President. My own view is that we should be a little more careful about assuming that there is an open-ended, undefined grant of power, of some sort, in that first sentence of Article II.

It is very difficult to find out exactly what it was that our Founding Fathers had in mind at the time, what they thought the "executive power" meant.

In 1936 the U.S. Supreme Court came out with a rather remarkable decision in the case of the United States against Curtis Wright Export Corporation, which is to be found in Volume 299 of *U.S. Reports*. The opinion was written by Justice Sutherland, one of the more conservative of that conservative corps of justices against which Franklin Roosevelt launched his infamous court packing scheme. Justice Sutherland came out with an extraordinary notion that when you look for the powers of the federal government in the foreign policy field, you find that they were not derived from the Constitution at all, but that they were received by a direct succession from Great Britain. To me it is a classic case of excessive judicial rhetoric. In any event, I tell my students, "read that case but please don't inhale it," because although the Justice Department occasionally cites that case *in arguendo* in a matter before the courts, I have never heard anyone in government, or in the executive branch, rely upon that case in any way, shape or form in order to derive executive powers from it.

But in any event, the executive power cannot be spelled out in terms of the powers of the British Crown in 1787. The Crown at that time had the power to make treaties. We took care of that in the Constitution. The Crown had the power to rule vast overseas territories, possessions, and colonies. We took care of that in the Constitution. So I think we have to live with the notion that there is no open-ended grant of whatever kind of power might be called executive power in our Constitution.

The role of the Congress in our foreign relations is very large indeed. Many of the things which a president wishes to do in the conduct of our foreign relations requires legislation or appropriations or both, treaties requiring the advice and consent of the Senate. Quite apart from the need for legislation, the question, "what does the Congress think about what we are doing or planning to do tomorrow morning?" is an extraordinarily important question for policy officers, including the president, to think about. Almost literally every committee of Congress finds that in carrying out its own responsibility it becomes involved in our foreign relations. That ranges from the Senate Foreign Relations Committee around to the House Committee on the District of Columbia. There is no single center in the Congress for the consideration of foreign policy as a whole.

On past occasions I have suggested that the rules of the House and Senate be changed to make it clear that the Senate Committee on Foreign Relations and the House Committee on Foreign Affairs should be entitled to call before themselves any matter pending before any other committee of the Congress in order to be able to comment on that matter from the point of view of our foreign relations as a whole. But that's a voice crying into the wilderness. There is no way in which the relations among the committees of Congress would make that possible.

The potentiality for impasse means that there is a special premium on communication between the two branches. If the separation of powers is a fundamental notion of our constitutional system, as I believe it to be, the other side of the same coin is the

constitutional necessity for comity between the branches, for
cooperation between the branches, and for due regard for the
reponsibilities of the other branch. That requires communication.
A typical method of communication is, of course, testimony
before committees and subcommittees of the Congress. That is
big business. Any librarian who tries to keep up with all the
published committee hearings in the Congress will tell you that is
a formidable task.

In my own case, in eight years, I appeared before committees
and subcommittees of the Congress hundreds upon hundreds of
times: thirty-two times in eight years on foreign aid alone; twice
each year on the authorization stage and twice each year on the
appropriations stage. Each committee, as a matter of its own
prestige, insisted that the Secretary of State personally come to
lead off the testimony. And each committee usually sent a word
down that they would be glad to have something fresh and new
about foreign aid. Well, you try to write thirty-two fresh new
speeches about foreign aid and you've got a little job on your
hands.

There are lots of committee hearings and each time you go to a
committee or subcommittee it takes at least two days of preparation ahead of time because in these hearings there is no rule of
relevancy. On each occasion you've got to be prepared to take a
question about any subject whatever from any member whatever.
So it is time consuming.

Beyond those hearings are individual conferences with, say,
the chairman and the senior minority member of important committees. Often congressmen who arrive in the House of Representatives as freshmen the same year will organize breakfast
clubs that meet once a month and you are invited to come down
to those occasionally, and you go. You pay very special attention
to congressional mail. We used to set a three-day turnaround time
for congressional mail to give it high priority. We didn't always
meet it in every case but we tried our best to do so.

I would go down, from time to time, to join with a senator or
congressman on one of those radio or television shows that they
put together in the special studio set up in the Capitol for that
purpose, which they would then send back to their home states
and home districts. I would do that on a nonpartisan basis.

Sometimes a senator or congressman would find himself with

a group of thirty constituents or so calling upon him, and he didn't know what to do with them. I would invite him to send those people down to the State Department. We would show them those extraordinarily interesting eighth floor quarters of ours. I would spend thirty minutes with them and I had a friend in that senator or congressman for life after that because that bailed him out of a tough situation.

These are examples of the many, many ways in which you try to communicate with each other. Now, some senators and congressmen obviously are more important than others. The chairmen and principal minority members of the Senate Foreign Relations Committee and the House Foreign Affairs Committee are very important people to you. The chairmen of appropriations subcommittees are extraordinarily important. The chairman of any committee which has oversight of the operations and organization of the Department of State is an important person. Sometimes those people, whatever department you are in, can exercise what can only be called undue influence in the performance of your own duties.

Sometimes special problems crop up. When the Kennedy administration first took ofice we were presented with strenuous objections from Mexico that we were in violation of an agreement reached some decades earlier about the quantity and quality of water which we were sending through the Colorado River to certain agricultural lands in northern Mexico before this river reached the gulf of lower California. When we began to move to see if we could bring ourselves into compliance with that agreement—because we ourselves thought that we were in violation—we had a very preemptory note from Senator Carl Hayden of Arizona saying, "Leave my irrigation districts alone." Now this was relevant because there were irrigation districts outside of the natural watershed of the Colorado River that were dumping their waste water over into the Colorado. That added to the pollution of the waters which finally reached Mexico.

Senator Carl Hayden came to the Congress the same year that Arizona, as a state, was admitted to the Union. In the 1960s he was not only president pro tem of the Senate but he was chairman of the Senate Appropriations Committee. Maybe as a matter of theory you can disregard that, but as a practical fact you've got a problem because the chairman of the Senate Appropriations

Committee has many ways in which to cause you to rue the day
when you, in his judgment, failed to be cooperative. So we had to
go to work on it. Of course, Carl Hayden was not immortal. We
did manage some filtration plants down near the border with
Mexico and we managed to bring ourselves, over a period of
time, into reasonable consonance with that agreement.

There is no substitute for communication. The Congress itself
varies from time to time and it is easier to communicate with them
at some times than it is at others. For example, in the early
sixties—I do not look back and say those were the good old
days—but in the early sixties, we could go down to Capitol Hill
and talk to four senators; Senator Russell of Georgia, Senator
Kerr of Oklahoma, Senator Humphrey of Minnesota and Senator
Dirksen of Illinios, and then go over to the House side and speak
to Sam Rayburn, and we knew what the Congress would or
would not do. They could tell us because they could tell the
Congress. Senator Russell could deliver twenty-five votes on any
subject whatever. The old fashioned kind of leadership system
has disappeared for quite a while.

LBJ used to refer to those five people I mentioned as the
whales in the Congress. As a political scientist I could make a
strong case against the whale system, but what case can you
make for 535 minnows swimming around in a bucket?

Some of those young turks who came in the late sixites and
during the seventies to upset the existing leadership system
themselves are now gaining some seniority, and they are concerned about how to restore the ability of Congress to communicate short of a vote.

When President Johnson—I think it was 1966—was getting
ready to go down to Punta del Este, Uruguay to attend a meeting
of all the presidents of the countries of the western hemisphere,
he thought it would be helpful if he had in his briefcase a
resolution of the Congress to give him some basis on which he
could negotiate or talk to these other presidents of the hemisphere. After some careful negotiation with the leadership of the
House Foreign Affairs Committee we got a pretty fair resolution
out of the House of Representatives. But when we went over to
testify before Senator Fulbright's committee about a similar
resolution out of the Senate, he told us that we shouldn't even be
there, that we shouldn't ask the Congress for any advance

expression of its opinion, that President Johnson should go on down to Uruguay and say whatever he wanted to say to the other American presidents and then come home and make whatever proposals to the Congress he wished, and then the Congress would take a look at those proposals and decide what to do. It isn't easy to extract prior recommendations from the Congress similar to the famous Fulbright and Vandenberg resolution calling for first, the United Nations, and then NATO. They are very reluctant to do that.

When you go before a congressional committee to testify, there are certain understood rules which you'd better have in mind. Sometimes new boys coming to town are not acquainted with those rules. The first one is you must never, never lose your temper before a congressional committee because if you do they will rip you to shreds. Second, you must never deceive them. This is not as easy as it sounds because of the limitations of time you have at those hearings. If the witness answers a question for more than about two minutes, whatever the subject, soon the chairman will tap his gavel rather gently and say, "I respectfully ask the witness to keep his answers short so that junior members of the committee will have a chance to ask their questions." In press conferences it is one minute. If you try to answer a question for more than sixty seconds, the fellows will start shuffling their feet and accuse you of filibustering to avoid more questions. So you are snatching at fragments of time in these hearings. It isn't easy to give any kind of considered, balanced weighing of the problem within the time that you have at your disposal. But you must never deliberately set out to deceive.

In Washington—this is a little bit of an aside—one soon learns the difference between men and women of honor, and the other kind. I'm glad to be able to report to you that my experience has been that the men and women of honor, rather than the other kind, are the ones who achieve influence, decisive influence, in places like the Congress. But you must never try to make a senator or a member of Congress look bad to his people back home. The question may be utterly stupid in your own mind but you must be very careful to accept it as a serious question, worthy of the most careful thought. Otherwise, you are in trouble.

One of the things that has complicated relations between the

Congress and the executive branch in recent years has been the
multiplication of congressional staffs. Some of you have those
numbers in front of you. I happen not to have them on the tip of
my tongue, but it is a several hundred percent increase in both
committee staffs and the staffs of individual senators and congressmen. They have reached the stage where certain bureaucratic syndromes begin to operate because these staff people have
to demonstrate that their jobs are important and worthwhile and
that they earn their pay. One of the ways they do that is by
tinkering with something. They contribute greatly to the oversight function and the requests for information from all over the
place, especially in the last few decades.

I noted with some alarm during the Carter administration a
little press article which said that the congressional liaison officer
at the White House was getting fifteen hundred telephone calls
per day. Even ten years earlier, ninety percent of those calls
would have gone to the departments rather than to the White
House. Some of the calls were from staff people, not senators and
congressmen, but staff people who wanted to be able to say to
their boss the next morning, "Oh, I talked to the White House
and they told me the following."

There was one method of communication that we began to use
in the mid-sixties which received, so far as I know, little or no
public attention but which I found to be invaluable, actually. We
organized a meeting at which we served coffee and donuts every
Wednesday morning at nine o'clock, down in one of the House
office buildings, to which every member of the House of Representatives was invited. At those meetings some senior officer of
the Department of State would come to talk about and take
questions on some important question of foreign policy. The
attendance varied from maybe sixty to three hundred, depending
upon who was coming and what the subject was. I had the strong
view that any individual congressman who attended those meetings regularly—and some of them did—would have a far deeper
and broader understanding at the end of a year of what was going
on in the world than would a member of Parliament from question
time in the House of Commons. This was very much appreciated
in the Congress, and it certainly was very helpful to us in
broadening the base of understanding in the Congress about what
was going on in the world.

These were closed meetings—the press was not invited—and

I don't recall that there was ever an indiscretion coming out of those meetings. We could be completely candid at those metings. But I don't remember a single indiscretion because the tradition was set that this was a method of communication which ought to be protected.

Well, that practice withered away during the seventies. I understand that when efforts were made recently to revive it that this time the resistance came from Capitol Hill. Members are just so busy. There are so many demands on their time that they can't find the time to invest in that kind of regular appointment.

Back in the sixties we offered the same arrangement to the Senate but the Senate turned it down. It was my impression that members of the Senate Foreign Relations Committee did not want the back-bench members of the Senate to become that much involved in foreign relations; they felt that that was the business of their own committee.

We need to give a good deal of thought to how we might be able to improve communications between the two branches. If we could sit down as Americans and talk about these things just by ourselves we could be more candid, and there would be very, very few secrets. The trouble is that in most of our discussions with each other, there are other very important audiences out there listening in to almost every word we say. Beyond the American people there are our allies, our potential adversaries, amd members of the so-called Third World. It isn't easy to deal with four audiences simultaneously. That is one of the reasons I rather enjoyed sessions with such committees because there you could be completely frank and candid without involving yourself with other diverse audiences.

As a matter of fact, about ten years from now it will be possible for the Miller Center to make a very interesting study. The Senate Foreign Relations Committee has in recent years been publishing slightly sanitized versions of its executive hearings, starting back in the Truman administration. Now when they catch up for a considerable portion of the television period, then it will be possible for somebody like you to compare the relative quality of discussion in executive session with that in open session. My guess is that you'll find that the discussion in executive session has been far more productive and useful than discussion in open sessions.

I mentioned earlier—and I'll be coming to your questions

shortly—this factor of time. I think most of us as citizens have no comprehension of the pressures of time upon our senators and congressmen. Hounds of hell are snapping at their heels with respect to time. That complicates the way in which one can communicate with them. They don't have the time to read carefully long reports. They don't have time to sit down and listen to accounts of the detailed situations in which 160 separate countries find themselves. It's a real problem.

I recommend that any administration proceed on the basis that partnership between the executive and the legislative branch is utterly essential in our constitutional system. Fortunately, that is made somewhat easier by the fact that, in the main, our foreign policy since World War II has been bipartisan in character. One must never expect unanimity; there will always be differences. But usually those differences do not fall along party lines.

As I said to some of you this morning, not once in all those hundreds of meetings with committees and subcommittees of the Congress did I ever see differences turn on party lines, Democrats on one side, Republicans on the other. But I think a president has a special responsibility to take the initiative to try to build bipartisanship in his foreign policy. I think of the working relation between President Harry Truman and Senator Arthur Vandenberg during the Republican Eightieth Congress, or between President Eisenhower and then Senate Majority Leader Lyndon Johnson for six of the eight years during the Eisenhower presidency, or between President Kennedy and President Johnson on the one side and Senator Evertt Dirksen on the other. He was a Republican leader of the Senate during the sixties. Those relationships are extraordinarily important and valuable. I would hope that a President would call down the bipartisan leadership of the Congress at least once a month to sit down with them, not necessarily to decide specific points, but for talk to try to build a consensus; to try to search out a common approach to the very complex and turbulent world in which we live.

The great, overwhelming majority of people in the Congress are honest and responsible people, concerned about the interests of our own country and the well-being of our people. Very often, if they can just understand what it is that is involved, it is not all that difficult to reach some kind of consensus. But a president must be willing to listen to people in Congress, to give thought to their views and to take them into account in reaching his own point of view.

When a new president comes to town there are two main sources of reservoirs of expertise waiting for him in the foreign policy field. One is the professional Foreign Service. The other is experienced senior members of the key committees of Congress. But a new president coming into town has a kind of edgy attitude toward both. These Foreign Service Officers were people who served, "those rascals, my predecessor." Or, "These fellows in Congress are potential adversaries; they will be out to get me." Well, they should come together in a more disarmed spirit than that in order to ask each other what is really best for the United States.

Now there are times when, in moments of crisis, the constitutional picture changes dramatically. I was with President Kennedy when he met with some thirty members of Congress, senators and congressmen, about two hours before he gave his famous television speech to the nation on the Cuban missile crisis. This is the first time many of them had heard about the missiles in Cuba, whereas we in the executive branch had had a week to work on it and think about what we thought ought to be done. This came as quite a shock to them. That was not consultation in the usual sense because realistically the only question before them at that moment was, "Are you prepared to support your country at this moment of peril?"

I think we ought to improve our conversations between the President and the leadership in between times so that we develop a kind of consensus which is so important to us. But I was very much impressed with the fact that during that meeting no member of Congress, senator or congressman, raised any question about whether President Kennedy had the constitutional authority to take the steps that he'd told them he was about to take, even though it would precipitate a very grave crisis. Indeed, the general mood of the meeting was that expressed to me by a senator on the way out. He said, "Thank God, I'm not President of the United States."

We have a difficult system. It takes enormous time on the part of those who are in it just to make it function. Its complications make it very difficult for the foreigner to understand, and many Americans don't fully understand it. But at the end of the day I must confess that I'm content with it, partly because our Constitution forces us to seek a consensus. It doesn't permit us to use to snap judgments or the whims of a passing majority just to act and run over everybody else. It requires us to seek a consensus, and I think there is great safety in that.

During the sixties there was a meeting in Washington of the NATO foreign ministers. I made arrangements for two of them to go out and visit the Strategic Air Command headquarters in Colorado. They went out, were taken underground and showed all the facilities and all the buttons to push and all that sort of thing. They came back through Washington and I met with them and I said, "What were your reactions to what you saw out there?" They looked at each other and smiled a bit and they said, "Well, we talked about that on the way home and we agreed that when we saw so much power we marvelled at the grandeur of American policy." Now, I think it is fair to say, despite Lord Acton, that this extraordinary power has not corrupted the American people. By and large, that power has been chained to the rather simple and decent purposes of the American people. There have been mistakes, frustrations and disappointments since 1945, but on the whole I suggest that American policy has showed responsibility and restraint and even generosity. We need not hang our heads in shame even though we should not brag about it too much.

Now, to the young people here, one final word. Let me remind you that, in this year of 1985, we have put behind us forty years since a nuclear weapon has been fired in anger, despite the many serious and dangerous crises we've had since 1945. We've learned during those forty years that the fingers on the nuclear triggers are not itchy, just waiting for a pretext to launch these dreadful weapons. I think we've learned that Russian leaders have no more interest in destroying Mother Russia than our leaders have in destroying our beloved America. That's no sure guarantee for the future; we have to be careful. I think we and the Russians must try to avoid playing games of chicken with each other to see how far each can go without crossing that lethal line. We ought to watch the level of rhetoric between the two capitals, and sometimes that concerns me. Bcause if that rhetorical level becomes too vitriolic over too long a period of time, there is always the possibility that one side or the other will begin to believe its own rhetoric and then we could have some problems. But I'm optimistic about the future because I've lived through some critical crises, and I bring away with me the impression that we humans at least are not idiots as far as nuclear weapons are concerned. I don't like all the Doomsday talk with which you young people are being besieged these days.

Well, I've talked perhaps a little longer than I intended but let's now take some of your questions.

*Question:* What do you think about President Reagan's SDI plan and his seeming reluctance to bring up the issue at the upcoming arms talks?

*Secretary Rusk:* First let me say that Mr. Reagan was not my candidate but he is my President, and I wish him well in foreign policy. We are all in this canoe together. We are going to come through these turbulent waters together or go down together. I have no interest in his failure in the matter of foreign policy, so if I disagree with him on a matter of this sort, it is painful for me to do so.

I support research on things like lasers, x-ray lasers, particle beams and things of that sort, partly as a hedge against a breakthrough in the state of the art by someone else, but also because I see no way to verify a ban on research. A man with a good mind and a slide rule might be the one who comes up with a critically important idea. But when we get around to thinking about deployment of such systems in outer space, then I become very much concerned. In the first place, this would require hundreds of billions of dollars. If some ten years down the road we find that these things are even scientifically and technically possible—if I were Jimmy the Greek I'd lay odds that they would prove not to be scientifically and technically possible—we have to assume that whatever we can do in such fields the Russians can do. Any idea that somehow we can get even a temporary advantage over them, I think, is illusory.

Then I go back to the inner rationale of the existing antiballistic missile treaty. We and the Russians agreed in the late 1960s that if we and they began to deploy antiballistic missiles, the inevitable result would be a multiplication of offensive weapons on both sides which could overwhelm the ABMs before the main strike came in. I myself have no doubts—to me it is as certain as the rising of the sun—that if we and the Russians begin to make some headway in devising such space defensive weapons, we should then be asked for additional hundreds of billions of dollars to bring in new offensive weapons which can penetrate or evade those space defenses.

I didn't see this in my local papers, but there was a story in the *Paris Herald Tribune* not too long ago saying that an official of the Pentagon had assured a congressional committee that if the Russians got these space weapons that we would have the offensive weapons which could penetrate or evade them. Therefore, we are talking about, what, a trillion dollars? Who knows? I would think that under those circumstances any fourth grade school child would say, "Why take that journey if you can possibly find some way to avoid it?" This would mean prepositioning commands to fire into computers and other forms of technology. I'd like to postpone that day as far as possible because I don't have that kind of confidence in technology. We lost three of our astronauts to the most expensive and well-tested technology we had. We put up some satellites that just disappeared into outer space; we don't know where they went. Two of our shuttle flights were aborted just seconds before they were supposed to lift off. (Mr. Rusk spoke before the Challenger tragedy.) The gap between promise and performance on the part of technology is a common, ordinary, everyday experience for us all. The rinsing cycle on the washing machine goes sour; the cycling on the dishwasher goes sour; the television screen goes blank, and it says "Stand by, technical difficulties." Only once in sixty years have I had a clock in an automobile that would keep time. So I don't like with such drastic things to put too much reliance upon computers and technology.

As I told a congressional committee some time ago, "To me the esthetics of blowing the arms race into outer space is repulsive. I want my grandchildren to be able to look up into the vast universe and reflect with the Psalmist that "the heavens declare the glory of God and not the folly of man." So you ask me about my views on SDI, there they are.

*Question:* Do you see Gorbachev as representing a new line in Soviet policy or do you see him as representing a more outgoing version of the same policy?

*Secretary Rusk:* I think it's a little too early to say. When Mr. Khrushchev left the scene we began to deal with a second generation of leaders in the Soviet Union. That itself made a difference. Up through Mr. Krushchev, communications that they sent to us were long and turgid and filled with a lot of ideological stuff that must have come out of a mimeograph machine and you had to look at it carefully under a microscope to figure out just what it was they were trying to say. After Krushchev's departure, their communications became shorter and to the point, pragmatic, and clearer. Sometimes they were tough; sometimes we didn't like what they said. But that itself was an improvement. Now we are beginning to see the third generation of leadership there. We have a tremendous stake in what kind of leadership that will be even though we may not yet know just how it will turn out. If Mr. Gorbachev and his generation will be practical, down to earth, concerned about the needs of their own people, ready to do business, then a good deal could be accomplished. But if they turn out to be another group of red-hot ideologues like the original old Bolsheviks, then we could have some problems.

I would hope that in the forthcoming meeting between Mr. Reagan and Mr. Gorbachev they would not waste time throwing ideological gambits at each other. If you hear that they meet for eight hours, divide that in half for interpretation, divide that in half again for equal time, and each one will have two hours to present his point of view in eight hours of formal sessions. They shouldn't waste time with ideological stuff. They should try to find common goals, common purposes, and common responsibilities, and then try to draw some conclusions from those. I hope they will do that. I don't know yet what it's going to be like. I just hope that Mr. Gorbachev won't do like Krushchev tried to do with President Kennedy and throw at him, in very harsh terms, an ultimatum on Berlin, threatening war along with that ultimatum, because that's no way to run a railroad.

*Question:* To what extent would you see the rise of a more aggressive press in the post-Vietnam-Watergate era causing more problems for the development of a bipartisan consensus on foreign policy than you feel is necessary.

*Secretary Rusk:* By the way, let me say at this point, that if anybody has a commitment and needs to slip out, don't worry about me. I've been walked out on by Mr. Gromyko and it won't bother me at all.

There is a question here about the press. Bear in mind that while I'm fanatic about freedom of speech and the freedom of the press—that's why I exercise my freedom of speech to criticize some of those who exercise the freedom of the press—that the very answer given by our friends in the press to the question, "what is news?" cannot help but result in a distortion of the picture of the world in which we live. I can tell you accurately, for example, that the overwhelming majority of international frontiers are peaceful. The overwhelming majority of treaties are complied with. The overwhelming majority of disputes are settled by peaceful means. But if that is not your impression, it is partly because normality, agreement, serenity are not newsworthy. Press people tend to concentrate on the controversial and violent. You have to watch that a little bit in trying to get the context of the news you hear.

There are other problems such as time. You only have a few breathless moments on radio and television news, limited inches of column space in the written press. So they too have the time problem as to what best to say within the limits that are imposed upon them. I've sometimes teased my friends in the press about the use they try to make of the phrase "the people's right to know." They are the last ones who ought to use that phrase because if they accept a notion that the people have a right to know then they have a duty to inform. They cannot accept a duty to inform without losing the First Amendment. They are stuck with the idea that whatever we have a right to know from them is whatever they decide to tell us. That's in the essence of the free press. But the press is more and more of a problem in the management of our foreign relations. It is a factor which has to be taken very much into account. Sometimes they can be helpful, sometimes not.

*Question:* What do you think about constructive engagement in South Africa?

*Secretary Rusk:* Well, I yield to no one in my abhorrence of apartheid. But having lived through a great many international conflicts and problems, I find myself regretting that all the forces I see at work now are moving toward confrontation. I don't see as much effort as I'd like to see in trying to find some solution. We would never have had a federal union had our Founding Fathers not made some fundamental compromises with each other to put this country of ours together. It seems to me that it is not beyond the reach of imagination and constitutional creativity for them to work out some arrangements with which all sides could live. But I don't see such processes going forward. I hope that they will begin shortly, but the more we criticize it from this distance, the more the whites down there are going to circle the wagons and develop a beleaguered laager mentality and be more resistant to the kinds of compromises that are going to be necessary. I'm a little sad that the movement is toward confrontation, in which a lot of people could lose their lives, rather than toward finding a solution.

*Question:* The United States' Constitution states how we should enter into treaties, but it doesn't say anything about how we should terminate or modify a treaty. What is Congress' role when the President of the United States acts unilaterally as in withdrawal from International Court of Justice proceedings, or when they propose withdrawal from the United Nations?

*Secretary Rusk:* The Supreme Court has often called the President the sole organ of our communication with other nations. In any event, he is the one who sends and receives diplomats. He is the one who delivers diplomatic messages on behalf of the United States. The question you raised was put to the Supreme Court by Senator Goldwater and a group of congressmen when President Carter sent a message to the Republic of China on Formosa making use of the one year notice in order to terminate our security treaty with the Republic of China. I talked to Senator Goldwater about that and told him that it seemed to me that that was one of those political questions which the Court would not and could not touch. We can't have a Supreme Court deciding whether or not a security treaty is in operation or not. The Supreme Court can't mandamus the President saying, "Send troops over there, you've got a security treaty." This is beyond their reach, and there are a good many constitutional questions which simply cannot be reached by the Court. The Court, in fact, held that this was a political question. At the same time, I suspect the Court was partly influenced by the fact that the Congress has passed legislation setting our relations with the Republic of China on Taiwan on a somewhat different basis. We were all ready to send an ambassador to the Peoples Republic of China.

I can't imagine how anyone could recall a President's notification to that government that we are invoking the one year notice for withdrawal from the treaty. Internationally, that is an official message from an appropriate authority of the United States government. The remedy is to go behind that and engage the Congress much more specifically in a confrontation with the President on that. But that was not done in this particular case.

There are always margins of possible contention around the edges of the Constitution about who can do exactly what. Generally speaking, my view is that a President can terminate a treaty. I would suppose that if he were under similar circumstances to notify NATO that we were withdrawing from NATO, that that could be grounds for impeachment, but we'll see.

*Question:* To what extent do you think that the constitution reflects reality in the running of the government? So many extra-constitutional bodies play a role in foreign policy.

*Secretary Rusk:* Well, the Supreme Court has pointed out from time to time that the Constitution is a living instrument and that it has demonstrated its capacity, if you like, to adjust to changing times, and I value that aspect of our constitutional system. I must confess that I myself am very conservative about amending the Constitution. We are soon to celebrate the bicentennial of the Constitution itself. I would not like to see us clutter up the Constitution with all sorts of provisions which can be done by legislation. Otherwise, our Constitution will soon look like the jungle that most state constitutions look like. I don't favor changes in the direction of compromising with parliamentary forms of govenment like some of my good friends are proposing these days. I don't think that you can make a case that these parliamentary systems have governed themselves any better than has our system. On the whole, I am relatively content with the way that our Constitution has worked, even though there are times when it is very difficult. I don't like these phony proposals.

For example, the proposed constitutional amendment to require a balanced federal budget. Now the President and Congress already have the power to balance the budget if they wish to, and they wouldn't dare pass such a constitutional amendment without an escape clause, "except in times of emergency declared by the President and the Congress," or something like that. So if the President and Congress are not prepared to balance the budget, they will simply live on the escape clause indefinitely. It is a sort of a phony issue to me when the power is already there. But there will be further controversy on this. Thank you very much; you've been very patient.

*Mr. Thompson:* We thank you, Secretary Rusk, most warmly and sincerely.

# Concluding Observations

The five thoughtful Americans who discuss foreign policy-making and discourse in the present volume are all both philosophers and practitioners. Each has had first hand experience in the public affairs arena. Their papers contain informed references to some of the crucial events of the second half of the twentieth century. They are also learned and well-informed in the literature of politics and policy-making.

This volume, then, falls appropriately within the mandate of the Miller Center, which is to study both the theory and practice of public affairs. It is addressed both to understanding and improving the workings of government, another responsibility assumed by the Center. It would be difficult to prepare a list of authorities better qualified to consider the issues they address. As such, this little volume is likely to be a work of enduring value for students, citizens and policymakers.